THE SCOUT'S COMPANION

Sonja Patel

THE COMPANION SERIES: COLLECT THEM ALL

The Birdwatcher's Companion
by Malcolm Tait and Olive Tayler

The Cook's Companion
by Jo Swinnerton

The Countryside Companion
by Malcolm Tait and Olive Tayler

The Curry Companion
by Sonja Patel

The Fishing Companion
by Lesley Crawford

The Gardener's Companion
by Vicky Bamforth

The Golfer's Companion
by Chris Martin

The History of Britain Companion
by Jo Swinnerton

The Ideas Companion
by Johnny Acton

The Irish Companion
by Brendan Nolan

The Legal Companion
by Vincent Powell

The Literary Companion
by Emma Jones

The London Companion
by Jo Swinnerton

The Moviegoer's Companion
by Rhiannon Guy

The Politics Companion
Edited by Daisy Sampson

The Sailing Companion
by Miles Kendall

The Shakespeare Companion
by Emma Jones and Rhiannon Guy

The Traveller's Companion
by Georgina Newbery and Rhiannon Guy

The Walker's Companion
by Malcolm Tait

The Whisky Companion
by Tom Quinn

The Wildlife Companion
by Malcolm Tait and Olive Tayler

SERIES EDITORS

Malcolm Tait, Emma Jones, Jo Swinnerton and Rhiannon Guy

A Scout smiles and whistles under all circumstances.
Robert Baden-Powell

First published 2007 by Think Books
an imprint of Pan Macmillan Ltd
Pan Macmillan, 20 New Wharf Road, London N1 9RR
Basingstoke and Oxford
Associated companies throughout the world
www.panmacmillan.com
www.think-books.com

ISBN-13: 978-1-84525-043-0

Author: Sonja Patel
Companion team: Tania Adams, Victoria Chow, James Collins,
Rica Dearman, Emma Jones, Mark Searle and Marion Thompson

1 3 5 7 9 8 6 4 2

A CIP catalogue record for this book is available from
the British Library.

Printed in the UK by Mackays of Chatham

FOR BEING PREPARED AND ALWAYS DOING THEIR BEST:

Anyone who has ever been a Scout.

Chris James, Hilary Galloway, Matthew Oakes and Rose Wells at The Scout Association.

Baden-Powell for paddling his own canoe, and producing a mountain of information along the way; Paul Moynihan and the Scout archive for guiding me through it all.

Lucy Hellberg, Jen Lewandowski, Charlie Birch and Rawia Edwards for adventures with tents.

Rob Tufnell and Guy Isherwood for their Scouting yarns.

FOREWORD

If Scouts are determined to do something, they will. Most of our Members are just ordinary kids who have a go – they love adventure, being able to look beyond themselves and find real friendship.

People ask me, why the Scouts? The main thing Scouting offers is an alternative community to school and home; a place where you can go where there is someone who is not judgmental. It allows friendship in smaller groups like a Six or Patrol, which is especially important if you have just moved from another part of the country.

One of the great ironies about Scouting is that it is a place of freedom, but ordered and structured at the same time. It's like when I tell my kids to tidy their bedroom; it's only so they can have the freedom to think. The same goes for adults: some people like a lot of structure and back-up; other people need freedom. A good organisation allows both of these things to happen.

Peter Duncan, Chief Scout of the United Kingdom

those boys. About [illegible] the Scouts [illegible] compromise [illegible]
all came [illegible] badges [illegible] the [illegible]
[illegible] children and [illegible] of [illegible]
[illegible] nights [illegible] sleeping [illegible]

I thought that Scouting was long behind me [illegible]
of [illegible] the civil war in Lebanon.

[illegible] my [illegible] as [illegible]
the [illegible] of [illegible] town of [illegible] to make [illegible]
[illegible] we were [illegible] and the [illegible]
We were [illegible] of the [illegible] of the [illegible]
[illegible]

We [illegible]
[illegible] a few [illegible]
[illegible]
[illegible]
[illegible]
the [illegible] we [illegible]
[illegible]
[illegible] men [illegible]
[illegible] how [illegible]

I suppose [illegible] only a few [illegible]
[illegible]

[illegible]

[illegible]

What [illegible]

[illegible]

[illegible] But I think [illegible]
[illegible] and [illegible] the world.

The [illegible]
but [illegible]
[illegible]
myself [illegible]
[illegible]
Scouting [illegible]

One hundred [illegible]
[illegible] 28 million [illegible]
around the world [illegible]
[illegible]

For [illegible]
[illegible]

INTRODUCTION

I loved being a Scout – the knots, the camping, the outdoor cooking, and all those Proficiency Badges in things like first aid, fishing and cycling. My most vivid childhood memories are of building rope bridges across the garden, mud ovens and nights spent sleeping out.

I thought that Scouting was long behind me when I found myself sent to report on the civil war in Lebanon.

Hearing of a ceasefire, my producer, cameraman and I ventured into the centre of the town of Tripoli to make our report. Unfortunately the truce broke while we were there and the most ferocious crossfire resumed. We were trapped in the middle of the city. The only way out was to hitch a ride with an ambulance transporting the wounded out of the battle.

We climbed in the back and curled up, to make ourselves as small as possible. After a few hundred yards the driver stopped the van and shouted at us to get down. He sank as low in his seat as possible; it looked as though he could hardly see over the steering wheel. We tried to make ourselves even smaller, then listened as he revved the engine, slipped the clutch and screamed off. As we rounded a corner, all hell broke loose. Bullets flew through the walls of the vehicle and bounced around inside. One spent itself an inch from my spine – I still have it on my desk as I write, a reminder how important a little luck can be in life.

I suppose the horror lasted only a few seconds, as we crossed no-man's land. It seemed like for ever.

At last, the ambulance came to a stop and the back doors opened. We piled out, our mouths dry with fear. Our rescuers led us into a building.

There was something instantly recognisable about it. The walls were hung with rope tied in demonstration knots and examples of different types of whipping.

'Why have we come to a Scout Hut?' I asked.

'Because we're Scouts,' they said.

There can be few enough Scouts who have put their membership to quite such dramatic purpose. But I think that the sense of social purpose is there in anyone who has worn the woggle.

The Scout's Companion will not tell you how to drive an ambulance. But it does contain such vital instructions as how to cook an egg in a potato or a fish in a newspaper on a campfire. (I used this technique myself a couple of years ago, and it produced the best fish I have ever eaten.) There's masses more: 'Things all Scouts should know' and tales of Scouting bravery.

One hundred years since Baden-Powell's first Troop set up camp on Brownsea Island, an amazing 28 million Scouts – in some 216 countries around the world – are still getting outdoors, attempting good turns and promising to do their best.

For all those who have so far refused to join the Jamboree, this might be the book to convert you.

Jeremy Paxman, broadcaster and writer and former Scout

AN A-Z OF ACTIVITY BADGES: A-B

This most up-to-date list of Scout Activity Badges proves there's more than one reason to join the Scouts. The list is provided in bite-sized pieces throughout the book so as not to get badge addicts too over-excited.

- Administrator
- Aeronautics
- Air Researcher
- Air Spotter
- Angler
- Artist
- Arts Enthusiast
- Astronautics
- Astronomer
- Athletics
- Basic Aviation Skills
- Aviation Skills
- Advanced Aviation Skills

ANIMAL MAGIC

The first ever Scout Jamboree, held in 1920, played host not just to a wealth of Scouts from different nations, but also to a veritable Noah's Ark of animals in a specially designated Boy Scouts' Zoo. An article in *The Scouter*, August 1920, enthused about the zoo in its write-up of the event: 'Great crowds throughout the whole week took the keenest interest in the animals, especially the lion and the alligator and the crocodile.'

Apparently the llamas were also of great interest, not having been seen by many people before, while 'the monkeys showed a very Scout-like spirit, making fast friends from the moment they were put together, although they had never met before, one coming from South Africa and the other from West Africa.'

An alligator from Florida and a crocodile from Jamaica (brought by one Scout who found it in the street and brought it in his pocket) were also said to have hit it off. Indeed, it was not a happy moment when the time came for these animals to say goodbye. However, some animals were presented to the UK, and others swapped between Troops, such as the tortoise that was presented to Scout Hales of Melchbourne (Bedfordshire) Troop by Scout Chas Bill of Jacksonville, Florida.

In this way, the animals became ice-breakers between Scout Troops around the world, and letters of enquiry were exchanged for years to come. Acquiring new friends and penpals has been a feature of Jamborees ever since.

 Year in the twentieth century that B-P set up the Girl Guides

CELEBRITY SCOUTS: JAMIE OLIVER

What this famous Scout did next...

Sadly the Scouts can't take all the credit for initiating Jamie's love for food: he attributes his parent's pub, The Cricketers, Essex, as the place where he truly learnt his basic cooking skills back in the 1980s. These were honed in France, then as head pastry chef at Carluccio's in Covent Garden, and famously, at the River Café where he was discovered as the next big thing by a TV talent scout. However, the 'Naked Chef' does have a penchant for cooking 'fresh ingredients' outside, with more than his fair share of quick-fix backwoods cooking recipes in his now extensive bibliography – most notably, the boy is a dab hand with a wood oven and tin foil. If he didn't get his Camp Cook or Chef Proficiency Badge in his Scouting days, then surely he should receive an honorary one now. Staying true to the Scout ethos, he's also one of our very best examples of what a 'good turn a day' can do. From Scout camp to projects such as Fifteen (where he trained potential ASBOs to be chefs in his restaurant) and Jamie's School Dinners (producing 'pukka' school lunches for kids who didn't know their broccoli from their hamburger) – B-P would be proud.

QUOTE UNQUOTE

The last temptation is the greatest treason:
to do the right deed for the wrong reason.
TS Eliot, poet

THEM WERE THE DAYS

Some more unusual Boy Scout and Girl Guide Memorabilia from vintage dealer www.johnrhoggarth.co.uk:

'Be prepared – HORLICKS!'
Advertisement from the 1950s

'Quick guide to stalking'
Article from *The Scout Annual* (1961) by Dan Gisbrook

'Fun with matches'
Article from *The Scout Annual* (1963) by Eric Franklin

'Making sheaths'
Article from *The Scout Annual* (1965) by Peter Bedford

'Boy Scout Hymn'
Band music card by Ralph Reader from the 1960s

'Job done! Bob-a-Job Week!'
Window sticker from 1967

Minimum age in years that B-P thought you should be to join the Scouts in 1907; today you can join at six years old as a Beaver Scout 11

THE CAMP COOK: EGG IN A POTATO

From *Backwoods Cooking – Practical Methods and Recipes*, a reprint of a popular collection that first appeared in *Scouting* magazine.

You will need:

- One large potato per person
- One egg per person
- Foil
- Teaspoon

Method:

1. Wash the potatoes and cut the top off each one.
2. Scoop out the centre of the potato, removing just enough to accommodate the yolk and white of an egg. Don't pierce the side.
3. Break an egg and pour it into the cavity in the potato and replace 'the lid' you initially cut off.
4. Wrap in two layers of foil and place in hot embers for about half an hour, turning it after 15 minutes.

Variations:

The egg can be replaced with grated cheese, minced beef and onions, corned beef, chopped ham, mushrooms, and so on. Be sure not to waste the excess potato – wrap it all up in two layers of foil with a large knob of butter and consign to the embers for 15 minutes or so.

The potato can also be replaced with a scooped-out orange.

CATAPULTED TO SUCCESS

The 1st Great Eccleston Scouts made it into the *Guinness Book of Records* by building the largest trebuchet in the world. Yes, you might ask, what is this trebuchet, and how hard can it be to make one? The record was, in fact, a year in the making. The device that had to be made was a large, medieval catapult, with a projectile of less than 20kg. The idea was first thrown into the arena when the Scout Troop built a ballista – a powerful crossbow that originated in ancient Greece – at a district camp. Then, with numerous trebuchets being built and tested over the years, the good people of Great Eccleston learnt when to run for cover. Size, horsepower and efficiency increased with each new trebuchet. The record-breaking trebuchet created a power output of 170.8kg, throwing a 2.26kg object over a distance of 75.6m. Let's hope they never have to use it in battle.

ONE SPOOKY SLEEPOVER

In June 2005, 33,000 Scouts, Guides and schoolchildren from across the UK participated in the annual BT Giant Sleepover. There were sleepovers in the Shetlands (the most northerly), sleepovers in the Falkland Islands (the most southerly), sleepovers in Northhampton (the biggest) and even sleepovers in the BT Tower (the highest). But the 4th Edmonton Scout Group took things to another extreme, and scared themselves witless at the same time, by bedding down in the London Dungeon. This was one night away where ghost tales around the campfire was definitely the order of the evening. Luckily, they survived the spooks and helped to raise thousands of pounds for ChildLine and other charities.

QUOTE UNQUOTE

I understand they deliberately teach these dashed Boy Scouts to cultivate their powers of observation and deduction and what not. Devilish thoughtless and inconsiderate of them, I call it. Look at the trouble it causes.

Bertie Wooster in *Carry on Jeeves* (1925) by PG Wodehouse

KEY SCOUTING DATES: 1907-1910

1907

August Experimental camp on Brownsea Island.

1908

January Part one of *Scouting for Boys* is published.

April First issue of boys' magazine *The Scout* is published.

1909

July First edition of adults' magazine *Headquarters Gazette* is published.

August Camp on training ship *Mercury,* leads to formation of the Sea Scouts.

1910

January Girl Guides is inaugurated.

March Silver Wolf badge added for any King's Scout who gets 24 Proficiency Badges.

September First annual census: 100,298 Scouts; 7,688 Scouters.

Age in years at which an Air Scout can go flying with the RAF (if they have been a Scout for at least six months and have achieved the Airman Badge) 13

KE LI LERNU ESPERANTON

In the July 1909 to December 1910 issue of *Headquarters Gazette*, B-P published a series of writings on how to teach yourself Esperanto. He was a big fan and believed that this phonetic marvel would be the language of a peaceful future: 'Esperanto is the greatest achievement in intellectual progress since the invention of printing... An international language must be quite as neutral as the Red Cross. It must tend to peace, and not war; its sway one of books, not bullets.'

Fellow fans can brush up on their Esperanto with a few key phrases 'that all Scouts should know'...

General Baden-Powell	*La Generalo Baden-Powell*
Scouts	*Skolto*
Chief Scout	*Konsilas Al La Skolto*
Teach yourself Esperanto	*Ke Li Lernu Esperanton*
The sun is shining	*La suno brilas*
The sky is blue	*La cielo estas blua*
I speak about a lion	*Mi parolas pri leono*
I see a lion	*Mi vidas leono*
Here is a haversack	*Jen estas tournistro*
I am a Scout	*Mi estas Skolto*
Give (to) me my hat	*Donu al mi mian capelon*
This belt is new	*Tui ci zxono estas nova*
Our tent fell	*Nia tendo falis*
The leaves of the trees shelter many small insects	*La folioj de la arboj sirmas multajnmalgrandajninsektojn*
The heaviest chest of all belongs to your squad	*La plej peza kesto el ciuj aparetenas al via tacmento*

SPREAD THE WORD

The names of just some of the Scout Troop magazines that have been set up over the years:

The Magpie .... 1st Hendon
The Howl .... 16th Bermondsey
The Rolling Stone .... 13th Carlisle (Grammar School)
The Bromley Scout .... 8th Bromley Rovers
The Kangaroos of St Bride's .... 56th City of Edinburgh
Coo-ee .... 23rd North London
Council Fire .... 1st Conway

 Age in years at which a Scout can now become an Explorer Scout

QUOTE UNQUOTE

So shines a good deed in a weary world.
William Shakespeare, playwright and poet,
The Merchant of Venice, Act V, Scene 1

SCOUTING AROUND: MELBOURNE, AUSTRALIA

In January 1912, Baden-Powell set off on his first world tour to see how the Scout Movement was developing. He recorded and later published his observations and musings. Today there are more than 28 million Scouts, youth and adults, boys and girls in 216 countries and territories. Of these, around 73,955 are Australian.

A very useful practice for Boy Scouts to learn is that of counting sheep... it's not quite so easy as it looks.

Sheep have to be counted very often on a run, and a boy who shows himself good at it come to the fore at once with the boss or manager.

The counter stands in a gateway and sends his dog to round up the sheep and to keep them moving through the gate while he counts.

The sheep don't dribble through one at a time–it would take you a month of Sundays to count them if they did; but two or three go timidly through, then there is a rush of a dozen together, then a few single ones scamper by followed by a whole mob pressing and squeezing together and so on. A beginner cannot count fast enough and soon gets confused, but after a little practice you begin to know about how many sheep are in a bunch by the size of it and you will be able to count by eights and tens at a time.

One shepherd told me that he taught himself to count sheep by practising with a bottle of peas. He used to let these trickle out while he counted them. At every hundred he undid a button of his waistcoat and began a fresh hundred.

At first he let the peas trickle very slowly, but when he got good at it he was able to let them run at a good pace, so that an onlooker would think it impossible to keep count. But if the onlooker stopped him at any moment and they added up the peas himself he would find that he had counted them correctly.

So when he came to count sheep he was able to do it quite well, and did not get chaffed by the old hands for making false counts as most tenderfoots do.

Robert Baden-Powell,
***Boy Scouts Beyond the Seas: My World Tour*, 1913**

READY, STEADY, SCOUT: PART I

Contrary to popular belief, Scouting was not established as an 'organisation' but rather more organic in its spread, picking up legions of fans along the way. The first UK Scout census of 1910 would count a phenomenal 100,000 members. Here, Baden-Powell tells his own account of how it all began, in 'How I started Scouting', *The Scout*, No 1, Volume 1, 18 April 1908...

I have suggested Scouting as a good thing for boys because I begun it myself when I was a boy, and I know that, if you want to enjoy life and get on, a great step towards it is to learn Scouting while you are young. And I am glad to see that, although the Boy Scouts have only been set going within the last two months, they are rapidly increasingly all over the country, and we even had letters from Burma, Gibraltar, and Canada asking for particulars, with a view to starting colonial branches.

My first beginning was 'in watermanship' – for we had in the family a small sailing-yacht, which we four brothers manned ourselves. This necessitated one of us being cook and crockery-washer, and I have not forgotten my first experience in that line. I had to cook the dinner.

First shot at cooking

Well, you know what it is when you begin as a Scout to cook your food – it is not quite success at first. Mine was not, either. The dinner was not good; I know it, because I ate the whole lot myself – not because I liked it, but because I had got to. My brothers could not eat it, so they made me do so, just as a reminder that I must learn to cook better.

I accordingly learnt a little about cooking after that from a cook at home, and I learnt from a baker how to mix flour and water and yeast to make dough for bread. I picked up a lot of Scouting when living in town by noticing what was in shop windows, and remembering the things and the names of shops and streets. I used to look at a map of the town and then go to a strange part of it and try and find my way to some church or other building without asking the direction, merely by remembering the map. I knew every short cut through back alleys and passages. I attended every fire that I could get to, and I made friends with firemen, and they taught me a lot about how to save people and how to put out fires.

There is plenty of Scouting to be learnt in towns, just as there is in the country or on the sea.

 Year in the twentieth century, that B-P set up the Wolf Cubs, for younger boys, using Rudyard Kipling's The Jungle Book *as inspiration*

TYING THE KNOT

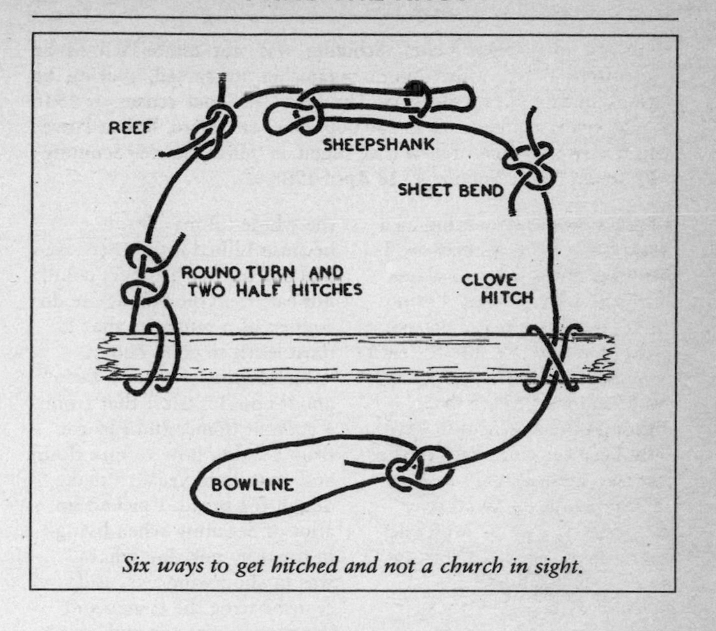

Six ways to get hitched and not a church in sight.

SCOUTS UNITED

Look hard at the three words below.
Can you find the missing link?

- Woodpecker
- Owl
- Peewit

Answer on page 153.

SCOUTING ENTERTAINERS

Billy Connolly • Jim Davidson
Ken Dodd • Val Doonican
Georgie Fame • Jimmy Logan
Gerry Marsden • Tom O'Connor
Joe Pasquale • Don Powell • Eric Sykes

Maximum age in years for Scout attendees at the 21st World Jamboree 2007; Scouts older than the 14-17 years must be Leaders 17

SAVE IT FOR A RAINY DAY

At a loose end? Here are two springtime ideas for older Scouts, from 'John Sweet's recipe for happy Scouting' in *The Scout*, 4 May 1950. What you do with each is up to you...

Idea Number One – Design and construct a hand-operated pile driver capable of driving a four-foot-six pile three feet in to the ground.

Idea Number Two – Design and construct a floating landing stage that will rise and fall with the tide without budging from its vertical position.

WE'RE JAMMIN'

Dates and places of all the World Scout Jamborees held over the past century:

1920	London, UK
1924	Ermelunden, Denmark
1929	Birkenhead, UK
1933	Gödöllö, Hungary
1937	Vogelenzang, the Netherlands
1947	Moisson, France
1951	Bad Ischl, Austria
1955	Niagara-on-the-Lake, Canada
1957	Sutton Coldfield, UK
1959	Laguna, Philippines
1963	Marathon, Greece
1967	Farragut State Park, USA
1971	Asagiri Heights, Japan
1975	Lillehammer, Norway
1979	World Scout Jamboree Year*
1983	Kananaskis, Canada
1987	Sydney, Australia
1991	Mount Sorak National Park, South Korea
1995	Flevoland, the Netherlands
1998/99	Picarquin, Chile
2002/3	Sattahip, Thailand
2007	Chelmsford, UK

* The 15th World Jamboree was due to be held in Iran in 1979, but was cancelled following the fall of the Shah of Iran in a coup that same year. Instead, simultaneous events were held worldwide so that no one would lose out.

 Year in the twentieth century that B-P set up the Rover Scouts for those who wished to continue Scouting over the age of 18

SCOUT SEND-UPS

For some people, the Scouts are better remembered in sketch...

Show	Episode
The Goodies	'Scoutrageous'
The Two Ronnies	'The Scout Jamboree'
The Goon Show	'The Man Who Never Was', 'Greatest Mountain in the World', and other episodes (with Peter Sellers as 'Bluebottle' The Scout)
Saturday Night Live	'Canteen Boy' (with Adam Sandler as a Scout who always wears a canteen around his neck; also starring Alec Baldwin)

QUOTE UNQUOTE

It always rains on tents. Rainstorms will travel thousands of miles, against prevailing winds, for the opportunity to rain on a tent.
Dave Barry, US humour columnist

SCOUTS FOR PEACE: BOSNIA AND HERZEGOVINA

Scouting is not just one big carefree Jamboree. With its inclusive approach to all nations, countries and cultures, the Scout Movement has helped many people in war-torn countries over the years, some of which were described in *Scouting* magazine, July 2000...

In 2000, Mustafa was 25 years old and grew up near Sarajevo in Bosnia. Before the war he had been a Scout. However, the Movement there was severely affected by the fighting. Activities stopped and many Scout leaders were scattered by ethnic cleansing and emigration. Undeterred, Mustafa managed to regroup Scouts from his district. He then also found that a similar group had also reformed in the other Serb part of the country. The two associations have since formed a federation and hope one day to have a single association. Taking inspiration from French and German Scouts who took part in the Jamboree of Peace following the end of the Second World War, Mustafa also organised to take the Sarajevo Scouts to the Central and Eastern European Jamboree – Peace 2000, organised by Serbian Scouts in Mlinska Rijeka. A brave move in a bid to emerge from the nightmare of war and move on.

HOW MAN BECAME CUB

...Father Wolf dropped with his haunches under him, ready for his leap. Then, if you had been watching, you would have seen the most wonderful thing in the world -- the wolf checked in mid-spring. He made his bound before he saw what it was he was jumping at, and then he tried to stop himself. The result was that he shot up straight into the air for four or five feet, landing almost where he left.

'*Man!*' he snapped. '*A man's cub. Look!*' Directly in front of him, holding on by a low branch, stood a naked brown baby who could just walk -- as soft and as dimpled a little atom as ever came to a wolf's cave at night. He looked up into Father Wolf's face, and laughed.

'*Is that a man's cub?*' said Mother Wolf. '*I have never seen one. Bring it here.*' A wolf accustomed to moving his own cubs can, if necessary, mouth an egg without breaking it, and though Father Wolf's jaws closed right on the child's back not a tooth even scratched the skin, as he laid it down among the cubs.

'*How little! How naked, and -- how bold!*' said Mother Wolf, softly. The baby was pushing his way between the cubs to get close to the warm hide. '*Aha! He is taking his meal with the others. And so this is a man's cub. Now, was there ever a wolf that could boast of a man's cub among her children?*'

'*I have heard now and again of such a thing, but never in our Pack or in my time,*' said Father Wolf. '*He is altogether without hair, and I could kill him with a touch of my foot. But see, he looks up and is not afraid.*'

Rudyard Kipling, *The Jungle Book* (1894). The characters described largely inspired B-P's Wolf Cubs and later Cub Scouts.

SCOUT AT HEART

Ten sure signs you're still hankering for those Scouting days:

1. You wear shorts even in the middle of winter.
2. You prefer a woggle to a Windsor any day.
3. You're always prepared (everyone else wants to catch you out).
4. You say 'Scout's honour' at any given opportunity.
5. This usually comes with a spontaneous three-finger salute.
6. Your love of the colour green is bordering on unhealthy.
7. You have a whole repertoire of knot-tying party tricks (which often clears the room).
8. You whistle while you work (this also often clears the room).
9. Badge-wearing is almost an obsession.
10. Your ideal bedtime reading is *Scouting for Boys* (which you hide under the bed).

 Year in the twentieth century of the 1st World Jamboree, held in London; also number of Scouts who took part in the first Brownsea Island camp

THINGS ALL SCOUTS SHOULD KNOW

In everyday life, both in town and country, there are interesting 'signs' to test your scoutcraft...
from *The Scout*, No 1, Volume 1, 2 May 1908

Phosphorus Safety Lamp

The first necessity for a night watchman is generally supposed to be a good lantern of some kind, but when he happens to be employed in a powder magazine this rather alters the case. You can make a light which combines absolute safety with sufficient illumination to read the time by a watch and other things in the following manner. Place a piece of phosphorus about the size of a pea in a small bottle of clear glass. Then fill the latter one third full of the best olive oil heated to boiling point and cork it tightly. When a light is required the cork should be removed to allow the air to enter, and then replaced. The whole of the empty space will at once become luminous.

NIGHTS AWAY

Tom and Larry had been blowing on the sticks for five days, but the flames still refused to come.

RAPPING AROUND RATIONS

A Scout had to make the best of limited food during the war by finding other things to eat, as illustrated by this latter-day 'rap', published in *The Scouter*, February, 1940.

I used to go to camp of late,
And never care a jot
What food I cooked, or what I ate,
So long as 'twas a lot–
Beef and mutton, pork and ham,
Sugar and butter and beans;
Bangers and dumplings, treacle and jam.
Cabbage or turnip greens.
Prunes and rice, or caviare,
Fish and chips from Harry's Bar;
Coffee or cocoa, chocolate, tea–
All of 'em went down well with me.

But now if off to camp I go
I'll have to take great care,
For coupons, which I have to show,
Must rule my bill o' fare.
Ration bacon, ration ham,
Sugar we count by the lump;
Shoulder or shin-bone, mutton or lamb,
Sirloin, brisket or rump.
Weight is easy, but woe is me,
Rations for meat are by £ s. d.
The Patrol must know, and the worry's mine–
What can I get for one and nine?

I'll have to read my woodcraft book,
And learn about the food
That grows, quite wild, by stream or brook,
In every field and wood.
Vetch and nettle, hip and haw,
Berries–both elder and black;
Acorns or chestnuts, cooked or raw,
Hazels and cobs to crack.
Roots or fungi, leaves or seeds,
All may help to supply my needs.
Dandelion as wine or tea,
All of 'em may agree with me.

22 *Date in February of Robert and Olave Baden-Powell's birthdays; it is now celebrated as Founder's Day by Scouts and World Thinking Day by Guides*

NOTES FROM THE FOUNDER

B-P on drawing, sculpture and art...

I like trying to draw. With me, drawing a picture is quite an exciting adventure, for I never know how it is going to turn out... I never learned to draw at school because it was an 'extra' and could not be afforded, but I tried to teach myself by studying and copying pictures by artists and noting how they got their effects.

...But what has this got to do with Scouting?

Why this – you will find, once you have taken to modelling heads, that you will look at every person you meet from a new angle. You will be noticing the set of his head, the form of his features and their expression, to an extent that you never did before.

You just can't help it. Your fingers itch to be modelling that nose or that brow with a lump of clay.

From such practice you will get to remember people when you have once seen them, and this, for a detective at any rate or for a Scout, is a very valuable accomplishment.

Robert Baden-Powell,
***Lessons from the Varsity of Life*, 1933**

SCOUTS UNITED

Look hard at the three words below.
Can you find the missing link?

- Tenderpad
- First Star
- Leaping Wolf

Answer on page 153.

A PHENOMENAL *FLEUR-DE-LYS*

Where is the world's biggest Scout emblem? In Mexico City of course. Thanks to the hard work of the Mexico City Scouts, the *fleur-de-lys* emblem – covering 1,000sq.m was created out of 1,155,670 used cans. Not only did this win another Guinness World Record for the Scouts, it also helped raise money for the communities of Chiapas (a region that was badly hit by hurricanes in 2005) and raise awareness about recycling. The emblem also marked an important date in the Mexican Scout Association's calendar: 2006 was their 80th year as part of the World Organisation of the Scout Movement.

Age in years of Olave St Clair Soames, when she married Robert Baden-Powell; B-P was 55 years old

QUOTE UNQUOTE

In the end I was Patrol Leader of the Dove Patrol. I was very keen on getting all my badges... my Woodworker's Badge, my Leather Badge and so on. If you were a Boy Scout, it kept you off the streets.
Stirling Moss, former racing-car driver
and former Scout

SCOUTS ON SCREEN

Just a few of the films that have Scouts featured in them:

14 Hours (2005)
Down and Derby (2005)
Men in Black II (2002)
Magic Power Scouts (1998)
Lawn Dogs (1997)
The Addams Family (1991)
Indiana Jones and the Last Crusade (1989)
Red Dawn (1984)
Airplane! (1980)
Follow Me, Boys! (1966)
Mister Scoutmaster (1953)
Joy Scouts (1939)
Mr Smith Goes to Washington (1939)
Good Scouts (1938)
Mind Your Own Business (1936)
Drum Taps (1933)
Boy Scouts Be Prepared (1917)
Charley Smiler Joins the Boy Scouts (1911)

HELP AT THE HAJJ

In February 2005, more than two million Muslim pilgrims were in Saudi Arabia for the annual Hajj. This requires visits to Mecca, Mina and Arafat where rituals must be performed along the steps of the journey. Every Muslim strives to make this pilgrimage at least once in his or her lifetime. Walking alongside them were more than 4,000 Scouts, ready to assist any pilgrims who had lost their way. In Mina, for example, there are 57,000 tents, and more than 20,000 buses to transport people – it is very easy to get lost. The Scouts also provided first aid and other emergency services to the pilgrims and were pleased that they had been of some assistance at this important time.

 The number in hours that Scouts have to try and stay awake for, at Gilwell 24 – an endurance test for Explorer Scouts

SCOUTING POLITICIANS

John Major • Neil Kinnock • Bob Cryer
David Evans • Peter Fry • Sam Galbraith
Lord Gormley • Ron Hayward • Eric Heffer
Lord Howe of Aberavon • Adam Butler • David Lammy
Tony Benn • Peter Mandelson • Lord Mason of Barnsley
Austin Mitchell • Hon Sir Charles Morrison
Lord Pitt of Hampstead • Lord Pym
Lord Rochester DL • Bob Russell • Lord Walker • John Ward
Lord Wilson of Rievaulx • Christopher Catherwood

PATROL NAMES AND THEIR PECULIARITIES: THE CUCKOO

As referred to in an enlightening series by JR Stanley (author of *Five Boys and a Master*) in *The Scouter*, January 1930:

- The cuckoo has never been known to visit before the end of the first week of April.
- The cuckoo's habits do not always meet with general approval.
- The cuckoo is generally freelance – here today, gone tomorrow – with a fresh mate in every port.
- The six or more offspring of one hen may each have a different father.
- The cuckoo builds no nest and has no settled home.
- The cuckoo is a big bird, as big as a pigeon but much slimmer, and when flying tall, appears unusually long.
- The cuckoo's plumage is generally grey with black and white barring on the breast.
- Its similarity in appearance to the hawk may account for the mobbing it sometimes gets from smaller birds.
- The hen cuckoo lays her eggs on the ground and transports them in her beak to some small birds' nests where the eggs are the same size.
- Target birds for nest pinching include the meadow pipit, wagtail or whitethroat.
- The cuckoo eats any eggs it finds in a stolen nest, and its young will eventually eject the rest.
- The cuckoo can be useful, in that it feeds on insects, especially on the hairy caterpillar which few other birds fancy.
- The cuckoo call, heard first in April, becomes hoards in June, and then ceases. Soon after, the cuckoo departs.
- The male bird is said to make the distinctive 'cuckoo, cuckoo' twin sound, but the female, more rarely, utters a tremelo imitation.

Maximum age in years for membership to Scout Network, the oldest Section in Scouting in the UK; the minimum age is 18

CRACK THE CODE

Can you work out the Morse code message below, without cheating by using the reference on page 39?

-... .- -.. . -. / .--. --- .-- . .-.. .-..

Clue: Who's the boss?

Answer on page 153.

GETTING LYRICAL

Scouts take their place in the music Hall of Fame...

Ramones –
'I Don't Want to Grow Up'
'I don't wanna be filled with doubt,
I don't wanna be a good Boy Scout.'

Jethro Tull –
'Thick as a Brick (Part I)'
'They're all resting down in Cornwall,
writing up their memoirs for a paperback edition
of the *Boy Scout Manual.*'

The Waterboys –
'All the Things She Gave Me'
'The moon's made of cheese,
And God is a Boy Scout.'

Pink Floyd –
'Welcome to the Machine'
'You've been in the pipeline, filling in time,
provided with toys and *Scouting for Boys.*'

SCOUTING SKILLS: TENTS

Skills to help you survive the wild, by Sir Ranulph Fiennes from *100 Years of Scouting* DVD (Endemol, 2007)

1. There are many different kinds of tents – make sure you choose the right one for the purpose.
2. Give your tent a good looking over and practise putting it up before you set off on your trip.
3. Think about where you are putting up your tent so you are protected from the elements.

 The age at which you are officially no longer a young person in Scouting

QUOTE UNQUOTE

Presenting kids' wildlife programmes, I've done a lot of things with wild animals that I really haven't done since the Scouts. Going after the tracks of animals, finding the spore of animals, taking apart owl pellets, shaking bushes to get the bugs that live in them out... There are certainly things that I did for the first time as a Scout that are absolutely central to my life now.

Steve Backshall,
wildlife presenter and former Scout

SCOUTS OF THE WORLD: PEACE-BUILDING IN RWANDA

Keeping the Scout Promise to 'help others', as part of Scouts of the World...

In 1996, genocide and terror spread throughout Rwanda and Burundi, prompting more than one million Rwandan refugees to stream into Goma. After a long, arduous, often barefoot walk from villages that had been 'ethnically cleansed', these people were faced with life in cramped camps that had insufficient water, food and shelter. The camps turned into death traps of disease, and even foreign aid workers who arrived to help were struck down by the consequences of the environment. One Scout, Gilbert, made a brave move to help. He invited all Scouts in the area to come together. More than 1,300 Scouts and former Scouts responded to the call and within days had buried 26,000 bodies who had fallen victim to cholera, starvation or died of stress caused by their journey. The Scouts also distributed food and clothing and helped form a backbone for non-governmental organisations working in the camps. But Gilbert also realised that some of the perpetrators of violence were Scouts or former Scouts. He resolved to try and make sure that hate between neighbours would not happen again. By setting up secret camps between Scouts in conflicting areas, he tried to instill a camaraderie that would mean no more Scouts joined any further calls to hate. Stopping just one Scout from joining in the violence was a step in the right direction. Gilbert and his team have kept their programme going strong since 1998; so far, more than 48,000 Scouts and 1,000 Leaders have been touched by its work.

RISING TO THE CHALLENGE

Scout Challenge Badges complement the programme of activities and have been developed to extend Scouts' skills and experience. The current challenges are optional and continue throughout the Sections, providing continuity from the ages of 6 to 25. They are:

- The Adventure Challenge
- The Community Challenge
- The Creative Challenge
- The Expedition Challenge
- The Fitness Challenge
- The Global Challenge
- The Outdoor Challenge
- The Outdoor Plus Challenge

CELEBRITY SCOUTS: BILLY CONNOLLY

What this famous Scout did next...

Scottish comedian Billy Connolly is not known to have had the most promising childhood, as his 2001 biography, *Billy*, would detail. Born in a poor tenement block, Billy tells of how he was abandoned by his mother, Mamie, at three years old, and brought up by his abusive aunt and father. Hopefully, his time with the Scouts brought some relief to him during this time, providing a chance to escape and a whole pack of lads on whom to practise his jokes. As a teenager he joined the Clyde shipyards, where he served his apprenticeship as a welder. An appearance by blues singer Pete Seeger on TV prompted him to buy a banjo, and a stint on Scotland's folk circuit (as part of the band Humblebums along with Gerry Rafferty) lent a musical edge to his repartee. Billy's big break came on the *Parkinson Show* in 1975, which led to his first UK tour 'The Big Wee Tour'. Armed with true Scouting spirit, Billy has always been game for a laugh even in the face of adversity, however, many years on the road would take its toll, and he became a heavy drinker. Billy's survival skills would really be put to the test this time, but blessed with the ability to bounce back and some true Scottish grit, he eventually kicked the habit in 1986. Every now and then Billy goes back to the Scouting theme (a favourite of comedians): in 2000, he played the Archangel Gabriel in the film *Gabriel and Me*, where he saved the life of a drowning Boy Scout. He also wrote and performed the song 'In the Brownies', which implies that Scouting is good but he'd rather be doing it with the girls.

 Number in millions of youth and adults, boys and girls in the Scouts around the world, in 216 countries and territories

A SCOUTING VOYAGE

Table of contents from *Paddle Your Own Canoe or Tips for Boys – from the Jungle and Elsewhere* by Robert Baden-Powell, 1939.

CONTENTS | PAGE

SCOUTING SKILLS: COLLECTING FIREWOOD

Skills to help you survive the wild, by John Ryder from *100 Years of Scouting* DVD (Endemol, 2007)

1. Wood that breaks easily is usually dry. Avoid wood that's been on the ground as it could be damp.
2. Go for a selection of thickness, some fine and some bigger branches. Use these to build the fire up.
3. Gather from far and wide so as not to disturb the environment too much.
4. Dead clematis bark, loosened by rubbing together as if washing socks, is also great for helping to start the fire.

Year in the twentieth century of the 3rd World Scout Jamboree in Birkenhead; its theme was 'Coming of Age' and 36,000 Scouts attended

THINGS ALL SCOUTS SHOULD KNOW

In everyday life, both in Town and Country, there are interesting 'signs' to test your scoutcraft...
from *The Scout*, No 1, Volume 1, 6 June 1908

Toast in Summertime

It isn't by any means necessary to have a glowing kitchen fire in order to make toast; it can be made at an oil or gas stove if the little device illustrated here is procured. The contrivance consists of a small square sheet of iron perforated with little holes, and can be obtained from any ironmonger. When toast is desired place the metal slightly above the flame, and in a few minutes it will be red hot. It then acts the part of a fire, and by holding a piece of bread or scone to it toast can be made to a nicety. The perforated part should be slightly larger than the opening of the stove in order to get all the heat possible.

KEY SCOUTING DATES: 1910s

1911

June Scouts on duty at the coronation of King George V.

1914

January First announcement of experimental scheme for Wolf Cubs or Young Scouts.

August Outbreak of World War I; war service is introduced.

1916

May Scout Jack Cornwell posthumously awarded the Victoria Cross.

September Cornwell Badge instituted.

December *The Wolf Cub's Handbook* is published and the Wolf Cub Section formally started.

1917

June New headquarters building introduced at 25 Buckingham Palace Road, London.

1918

August The name of the Senior Scout Section is changed to Rover Scouts.

1919

January Gilwell Park purchased for use as a Scout campsite and adult training centre.

 Number of boys who won a place in Scouting *magazine to take part in Baden-Powell's second experimental camp at Humshaugh, Northumberland*

QUOTE UNQUOTE

You can't catch a cub without going into the tiger's den.
Ancient Chinese proverb

SCOUTING SPORTS PERSONALITIES

Brendon Batson – *footballer* • David Beckham – *footballer*
Paul Bracewell – *footballer* • Trevor Brooking – *pundit*
Gordon Bulloch – *rugby player* • Brian Clough – *football manager*
Ian Clough – *mountaineer* • Nigel Clough – *footballer*
Tim Foster – *rowing gold-medalist* • Martin Keown – *footballer*
Christopher Lambert – *athlete* • Robert Lee – *footballer*
Sammy Lee – *footballer* • Graeme Le Saux – *footballer*
Malcolm MacDonald – *football manager*
Derek Mountfield – *footballer* • Andrew Murray – *tennis player*
Peter Oosterhuis – *golfer* • Michael Owen – *footballer*
Gordon Pirie – *athlete* • Mark Ramprakash – *cricketer*
Bobby Robson – *football manager* • David Seaman – *goalkeeper*
Lee Sharpe – *footballer* • Gareth Southgate – *footballer*
Graham Stuart – *footballer* • Tommy Taylor – *football manager*

CARTOON CAPERS: DONALD DUCK

Seems Scouts have had something to get animated about for nearly 70 years. First up, Scouting capers from Donald Duck...

***Good Scouts* (1938)**
Donald gets chased by a bear after falling into a pot of honey, thanks to the too tight bandaging of his nephew-strong Scout Troop.

***Sea Scouts* (1939)**
Donald has a run-in with a shark after taking his Scout Troop on a large sailboat where the sailing is anything but smooth.

WHERE AM I?

A Scouting riddle...

A Scout left his campsite one morning to go for a three-mile hike. He headed due south for one mile then rested. After his break he hiked due west for one mile, then stopped to eat lunch. After lunch he hiked due north for one mile and arrived back at his campsite.

Where was he camped? At the North Pole of course.

Year in the twentieth century of the 1st Rover Scout Moot – a meeting of World Rover Scouts – held in Kandersteg, Switzerland

THE OTHER BADEN-POWELL

When Robert Baden-Powell died in 1941, his memory was kept alive not just by the Scout Movement but also by a young boy from the Varre e Sai district of Brazil. Born 6 August 1937, 'Baden the Brazilian' was named after his grandfather – a musician and conductor – and his father before him, the latter being a staunch admirer of the Boy Scouts founder, as well as being dedicated to the abolition of slavery in Brazil. Like Baden-Powell of Gilwell, the young Baden was to find international fame – but of a slightly different kind. This Baden grew up to be renowned as one of Brazil's finest musicians, fusing jazz, classical and afro styles.

Following in the footsteps of his musician father he took private guitar lessons from Jaime Florence, a guitar professor who introduced him to the work of Spanish masters like Francisco Tárrega and Andres Segovia. Baden first presented himself as guitar soloist at Renato Murce's show Papel Carbono at the tender age of nine. After high school he joined the cast of Rádio Nacional as accompanist, travelling throughout Brazil. He then joined Ed Lincoln's trio, playing jazz at the Plaza nightclub in Copacobana – a popular hangout for musicians and writers – where he was noticed by the composer Antonio Carlos Jobin.

Baden's first major hit was 'Samba Triste' in 1956, but this success was cemented after meeting Vinicius de Moraes, a composer, poet and singer. Their collaboration produced more than 50 songs. The pair also became immersed in bossa nova – a stylistic reworking of traditional samba rhythms, a big hit in the late 1950s and 1960s. Further popularity came with the release of 'Samba da Bénção', or 'Samba Saravah' as it appeared on the soundtrack for Claude Lelouch's movie *Un Homme et Une Femme*.

After a time spent on the idyllic Brazilian isle of Bahia, the afro element was introduced into Baden's music. This is most notable in 'Berimbau', where the sound of the bow used in capoeira (a Brazilian martial art) is subtly recreated on the guitar.

From there, stints in Paris (following a mass exodus after a military coup in Brazil), introduced him to some of the musical world's greats, including Stan Getz and Thelonious Monk. Teaming up with them also brought him acclaim in the US but Baden was never to live there. Instead, he moved to the city of Baden-Baden in 1983, using his new aptly-named home as a base for playing at jazz clubs in Europe, Japan and the US.

When he finally moved back to Brazil, his popularity there had dwindled a little, but he still continued to play the clubs (although some felt his style had toned down after he became an Evangelical Christian). His death in 2000 left two more Baden-Powells to the world: Philippe and Louis-Marcel Baden-Powell de Aquino, both of Rio de Janeiro.

NIGHTS AWAY

'Not another burnt kebab,' thought Gordon.

PADDLE YOUR OWN CANOE

For a man 'tis absurd to be one of a herd,
Needing others to pull him through;
If he's got the right grit he will do his own bit
And paddle his own canoe.
He'll look without dread at the snags on ahead,
Wine, women and highbrows too;
He won't run aground but will work his way round,
With a smile, in his own canoe.

Chorus: So love your neighbour as yourself
As the world you go travelling through
And never sit down with a tear or a frown
But paddle your own canoe.

A motivating mantra to help you on life's way,
by Robert Baden-Powell, in *Rovering to Success: A Book of Life-Sport for Young Men*, 1930

Year in the twentieth century in which the 4th World Scout Jamboree was held in Gödöllö, Hungary; some 25,000 Scouts from 35 nations attended

KEY SCOUTING DATES: 1920s

1920

July	1st World Scout Jamboree (30 July to 8 August) held at Olympia, London. Scouts camp in Richmond Park.

1921

September	First Gilwell Reunion; at the Scouts' Own an Arab reads from the Qu'ran and a Hindu recites the Scout Law.

1922

June	Baden-Powell's *Rovering to Success: A Book of Life-Sport for Young Men*, a handbook for Rover Scouts, is published.
September	A posse of welcome for the Prince of Wales at Alexandra Palace, London, is attended by 20,000 Wolf Cubs, 43,000 Scouts and 2,000 Rover Scouts.

1923

January	*Headquarters Gazette* changes its name to *The Scouter*.
July	The woggle is introduced for holding the scarf.

1924

August	Imperial Jubilee is held at Wembley and 34 parts of the empire are represented. Second World Scout Jamboree held later in Denmark.

1926

July	Presentation at Gilwell Park of the Bronze Buffalo by the Boy Scouts of America.

FOILED AGAIN

Household aluminium foil has many uses in a backwoods cooking environment. Use it as a:

- **Disposable washing-up bowl** – dig a small hole in the ground, line it with two thicknesses of foil and fill with water.
- **Drinking cup** – mould two layers of foil around an old can or large stone and crimp the edges after removing the can or stone.
- **Strainer** – as above, but pierce holes in the bottom of the cup.
- **Frying pan** – made with a green forked stick and a 'bowl' of foil.
- **'Boil in the bag'** – fold foil into a bag and use to boil eggs or cook meat and vegetables.

 Number of countries represented at the 1st World Scout Jamboree; some 5,330 Scouts took part at the event in Olympia, London

THE CAMP COOK: COWBOY DINNER

From *Backwoods Cooking – Practical Methods and Recipes*, a reprint of a popular collection that first appeared in *Scouting* magazine.

You will need:

- One small potato and one small onion
- A few green beans
- Four slices of bacon
- About 50g of minced beef

Method:

1. On a piece of foil, approximately 20cm square, lay two strips of bacon about 2cm apart.
2. Place some green beans across the bacon. Add thin slices of onion.
3. Next, place two slices of potato, the minced beef, some more onion, and then the remainder of the potato.
4. Finally, put the remainder of the green beans on and cover the lot with the last two slices of bacon.
5. Fold any ends of bacon over in order to cover the sides of the food 'pile' and carefully side the whole dinner into a foil bag.
6. Place in hot embers, cooking for around 15 minutes on each side.

NOTES FROM THE FOUNDER

B-P on The Scout Promise…

So I inflicted on the Scout, a solemn little Promise, easier to keep than an Oath, in which he engaged to do HIS BEST to:
Do his Duty to God and to the King (N.B.-Not merely to be loyal, which implies a state of mind, but to DO something).
Do a good turn to somebody every day (i.e. Duty to his Neighbour).
Obey the Scout Law.

The number in a Pack or Troop should preferably not exceed thirty-two. I suggest this number because in training boys myself I found that sixteen was about as many as I would deal with-in getting at [and bringing out the individual character in each.]. I allow for other people being twice as capable as myself and hence the total of thirty-two.

The term Scoutmaster was no new one. It was an old English title used by Cromwell, who had "Scoutmasters" in his Army, and his Intelligence branch was under the direction of a "Scoutmaster-General."

Robert Baden-Powell
***Lessons from the Varsity of Life*, 1933**

Time in minutes within which a Scout must swim 1,000m using any three recognised strokes, to help gain the final stage of their Swimmer Badge

AND A ROVER YOU WILL BE...

The Rover Scouts were established in 1918 in the UK as a Section of the Movement that had no upper age limit. In 1956 this was fixed at 24. Rover Scouts have since morphed, first into Venture Scouts and then into the current Explorer Scouts and the Scout Network. If Rover Scouts were around today you might see them doing some of the following...

Tracking: Of men, animals, wheels etc, and the reading of information therefrom.

Fire-making: In the way that a tramp or Red Indian does it, and not as you would do for a jubilation on Guy Fawkes Day. A mere handful of red-hot embers will do all the cooking needed. (Take note that one ex-Scout who, during the war escaped from a German prison, managed to subsist and keep himself concealed largely thanks to what he had learned as a Boy Scout, especially in the matter of hiding his tracks and of cooking his grub over a diminutive fire.)

Cooking: With what the Red Indians call a chiploquorgan, or bent osier, to hold your 'billy' over the fire, and a mulquagan or forked stick, round which dough can be twisted for bread and upon the points of which your slabs of meat can be fixed for roasting.

Carrying a tent: Not a canvas tabernacle, but the light-weight bivouac that is used largely by practical campers, and can almost be carried in one's pocket.

Knot-tying: Like the use of needle and thread, this is a necessary bit of knowledge for a camper.

Wielding an axe: And knowing not only how to use the axe but how to take care of it.

Map-reading: Finding one's way by map, land-marks, compass, stars and direction of winds, etc. This is as interesting as it is essential.

Sporting a rucksack: As its load teaches you how little you have to do with when hiking.

Practising eyesight: By practice your eyesight is strengthened to a notable degree, especially if you are town bred and have never had occasion to look more than 50 yards ahead of you.

Aiding hearing: Strengthen hearing by listening to sounds by night; one's sense of smell is also invaluable for finding one's whereabouts or the presence of other people at night.

Judging distance: This is an art developed by practice when hiking.

Weather-reading: Invaluable to a hiker, who soon gains it by continual observation.

Reciting nature lore: This becomes second nature to the outdoor man and gives him a new interest and joy in life.

Improvising camp utensils: Sometimes apparatus has to be improvised, and this teaches one hardiness and resourcefulness.

Adapted from Robert Baden-Powell's *Rovering to Success: A Book of Life-Sport for Young Men*, 1930

36 *Number of activities from which Cub Scouts could choose in the Developed Arrow Scheme, a modified award scheme that ran from 1978 to 1990*

WHAT A JOB

Some typical entries from 'Bob-a-Job' job cards, as described in *The Scouter*, 1950...

'Looking after an old lady for three weeks' – a good turn indeed.
'Slug catching – two hours' – by a small Wolf Cub.
'Cleaning windows – one guinea' – by a County Commissioner.
'Rescuing a boy's trousers from mid-stream'
– by a Patrol of Sea Scouts.
'Unpacking 1,440 eggs for a grocer without breaking one'
– by another Wolf Cub.

NIGHTS AWAY

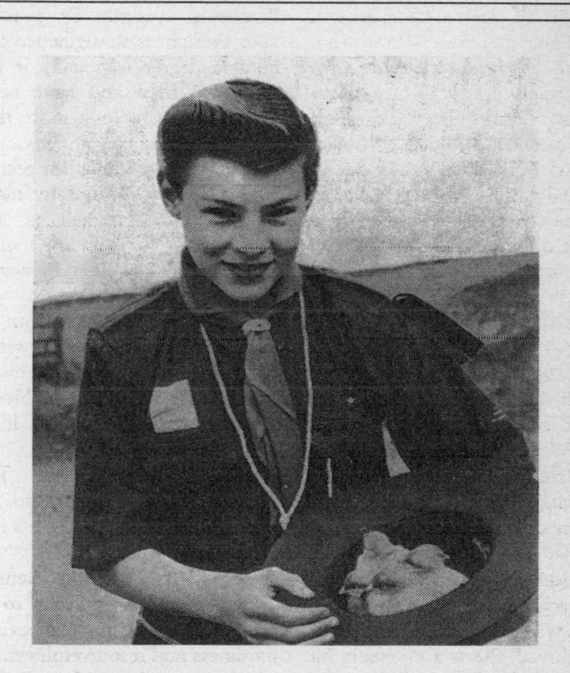

Two years in the Moorhen Patrol had left James a little confused.

THE TALLEST BOY SCOUT IN THE WORLD

The Scouts have broken numerous world records, but the tallest story belongs to Robert Pershing Wadlow. He was born in 1922 in Alton, Illinois, and at 8ft 11.1in (2.72m) he qualifies as the tallest person ever recorded in history. At the time of his death in 1940, his height dictated that he weighed 490lb (222kg). Sadly, Robert's outlandish growth was due to an over-active pituary gland, and with today's medical technology he could have been allowed a more normal growth pattern. Determined to make the best of things, however, Robert did not let his size come in the way of his enthusiastic stamp collection or passion for photography. He also became the world's tallest Boy Scout at 7ft 4in (2m), when he was 13 years of age. His weight was 270lb (122kg) and, according to the Alton Museum of History and Art, it took 14 yards (13m) of 36in-wide (91cm) material to make his Boy Scout uniform.

QUOTE UNQUOTE

Flout 'em, and scout 'em; and scout 'em and flout 'em;
Thought is free.
William Shakespeare, playwright and poet,
The Tempest, Act III, Scene 2

DIG, DIG, DIG!

Following the Minister of Agriculture's appeal for all to 'grow more food', an article appeared in *The Scout*, 14 October 1939, urging Scouts to do their bit for the war effort. The Scouts rose to the challenge and, in this way and others, helped to make life a little easier until peace reigned once more...

'Our ultimate victory may depend in no small measure upon the way in which the people of this country respond to the Government's appeal to grow as much food as possible in every garden and on every allotment and every smallholding throughout Great Britain.

'So, here is a chance for Scouts who have no definite National Service job to play their part in ensuring our safety and the success. It is really wonderful how much food you can grow in a small garden. On a plot of ground measuring 10 yards by 30 yards you can grow about £10 worth of food, enough to provide a family of four with vegetables for at least six months.'

CRACK THE CODE

Morse Code – the next big text message trend...?

.-	A	-.	N
-...	B	---	O
-.-.	C	.--.	P
-..	D	--.-	Q
.	E	.-.	R
..-.	F	...	S
--.	G	-	T
....	H	..-	U
..	I	...-	V
.---	J	.--	W
-.-	K	-..-	X
.-..	L	-.--	Y
--	M	--..	Z

NOTES FROM THE FOUNDER

B-P on Proficiency Badges...

Boys are not alone in their love of badges to wear. I have heard of grown-up men who would risk, and have risked, their lives to get a medal.

So, although it may be counted immoral to appeal to this touch of vanity in the boy, we have instituted badges as proficiency which any Boy Scout can earn by taking the trouble to qualify and pass tests for them. These badges are awarded for proficiency in such things as carpentry. Swimming, ambulance work, etc., etc. There are nearly sixty different subjects, among which every boy should be able to find one more suited to him.

Thus he is encouraged to take up a hobby and a lad with hobbies will as a rule not waste his life.

Moreover, there is only one standard by which a boy is judged as qualified for a badge, and that is the amount of effort he puts into his work. This gives direct encouragement to the dull or backward boy–the boy in whom the inferiority complex has been born through many failures. If he is a trier, no matter how clumsy, his examiner can accord him his badge, and this generally inspires the boy to go on trying till he wins further badges and becomes normally capable.

The prime badge is the Cornwell Badge for Courage, instituted in memory of ex-Scout Jack Cornwell, VC, killed on board the Chester at the Battle of Jutland in the Great War.

Robert Baden-Powell,
***Lessons from the Varsity of Life*, 1933**

PATROL NAMES AND THEIR PECULIARITIES: THE OTTER

As referred to in an enlightening series by JR Stanley (author of *Five Boys and a Master*) in *The Scouter*, January 1930:

- An otter's body is elongated, somewhat like a stoat.
- An otter has no marked constriction in the region of the neck, which enables it to glide easily through the water.
- An otter's limbs are short, the toes webbed, and the small claws curved and blunt.
- An otter's close, thick fur readily throws off the water.
- An otter's ears are small and the teeth are formed to catch and retain the slippery fish on which he chiefly feeds.
- An otter eats water voles, frogs and even moorhens.
- An otter's body can reach a length of 26in (66cm), while the tail may be 16in (41cm) long.
- Otters often form a small patrol in order to enclose a shoal of fish, which they often kill wantonly.
- Otters almost invariably consume their captures in their lairs.
- Otters are shy, retiring creatures, spending most of the day in their burrows.
- Otters have two or three young in the spring, and these are called kits.
- Otters' kits are born blind and remain so for about 80 days.
- An otter's haunt is its 'hole', its tracks 'seals', and its surface trail of bubbles when breathing under water 'ventings'.
- The sound associated with the otter is a sharp, rasping call 'kerk', like that of the moorhen.
- The Patrol call for an otter is given as 'Hoi-oi-oich'.

THINGS ALL SCOUTS SHOULD KNOW

In everyday life, both in town and country, there are interesting 'signs' to test your scoutcraft...
from *The Scout*, No 1, Volume I, 23 May 1908

How to act with a drowning man

There's no harm in knowing just how to tackle a drowning man, although one may never be called upon to act on the knowledge. The great thing is to be out of the drowning man's way in case he struggles, and another important thing is to have as much freedom for one's own limbs as possible. So long as the head is sustained above water there is no need to attempt to support more of the body; then swim backwards by vigorous leg strokes till safety is reached.

 Year in the twentieth century in which artist Norman Rockwell presented the painting A Scout is Reverent; *he was well known for his depictions of Scouts*

WHOSE BADGE IS IT ANYWAY?

You might have a full arm of new badges. Or you may be taking a trip down memory lane. But can you guess what this Cub Scout Proficiency Badge is for?

a) Dragon boating
b) Fire breather
c) Anger management

Answer on page 153.

HUNGRY LIKE THE WOLF CUB

Backwoods cooking for beginners – not to be attempted by adults unless under the expert supervision of a qualified Cub Scout:

Tarzan steak
Blow the white ash from your glowing coals and place the steak directly onto the coals, cooking for about five minutes per side.

Fried eggs
Bury a flat stone in the hot coals and, when hot enough (a drop of water on the stone will sizzle if the stone is hot enough to cook on), sweep the ashes off. Crack an egg directly onto the stone, using a surround of greensticks to contain the egg if necessary. Burgers, sausages and bacon can also be cooked in this way.

Twists
Mix flour, water and a pinch of salt together to form a thick dough, adding raisins and sultanas if the budget will stretch that far. Take a piece of this dough and roll it into a snake-like length, wrapping it around a greenstick (with the bark removed). Support over glowing embers, turning occasionally until the outside turns golden brown.

Baked potatoes
Encase a medium-sized potato in 1in-thick (2.5cm) layer of mud or clay and place in hot embers for about 25 minutes.

GIRLS WILL BE BOYS

Some feedback from the members of the 1st Orwell Cub Scout Pack (Cambridgeshire) – in their own words, spelling and all – regarding the admission of girls to Scouting, as reported in *Scouting* magazine, November 1990.

Dear Sir,
I do not think girls should go to cubs becoce it was made for boys and we go to get away from girls and girls are not very strong.
Yours sincerely
Jon Miller

Dear Sir,
I heard if your letter threatening to let girls into Cubs and Scouts. There is one complaint about this. Girls already have Brownies and Guides. Apart from that they are pretty stupid. But apart from that. PLEASE LET THEM JOIN.
Yours hopefully
Anonimus

Dear Sir,
I would not mind if girls come to our Cub Pack, because we will get to no them more and more in the village and at cubs. I would like girls to come to cubs because you could get a girl-friend.
Please let them come.
Yours sincerely
Joe Aliker

Dear Sir
I think that the girls should be able to join cubs and boys should be able to join Brownies if some boys don't like to rough games they would not be able to do anything on friday night Some girls like to think as they are boys and play rough games I wouldn't mind besides there all human.
Yours sincerely
Ross Lenndrel

Dear sir,
I do! want girls to join cubs because you can see your girlfriends more.
Yours sincerely
Christopher D

TWO SUSPECT SCOUT OUTINGS

Uncovered in *Scouting* magazine, 1990...

1. Members of the 14th Northvale Scout Group from Shadwell in Leeds prepared for a meal for a chief inspector at West Yorkshire's Police Driving School. The chief inspector then had to eat the meal whilst being driven around the skid pan in a police car.
2. Members of the 31st Wakefield (St Anne's) Cub Scout Pack visited the Central Police Station in Leeds and were locked in the cells after having their fingerprints taken.

 Year in the twentieth century in which former Chief Scout George Purdy was born; he held the post from 1996 until 2004

KEY SCOUTING DATES: 1930s

1932

October	The first Gang Show is produced by a 'Holborn Rover'. (He is later revealed as theatre producer Ralph Reader.)

1935

November	A new design for the Thanks badge is approved to replace the old swastika design following the Nazi Party's adoption of the same emblem.

1937

November	Royal Command Performance of the Gang Show.

1938

February	The fourth Scout Law is amended to read: 'A Scout is a friend to all and a brother to every other Scout, no matter to what country, class or creed the other may belong.'

1939

February	National Service Badge is introduced for Scouts, Rovers, Scouts, Old Scouts and Scouters.
September	Germany invades Poland.

SCOUTING AROUND: JAPAN

In January 1912, Baden-Powell set off on his first world tour to see how the Movement was developing. He recorded and later published his observations and musings. Today there are more than 28 million Scouts, youth and adults, boys and girls in 216 countries and territories. Of these, around 195,370 are Japanese.

As we steamed across the great bay to the harbour of Yokohama, a small steamer 'dressed' with flags came out to meet our ship and escort us. The Union Jack was flying conspicuously at the top of the mast; the deck was crowded with Boy Scouts. So the Scouts of Yokohama had come out to welcome me.

...I went and saw a lot of them at their daily practice of fencing with bamboo sticks and practising jiu-jitsu to make themselves strong and active and good-tempered. I say good-tempered, because it is very like boxing, you have to take a good many knocks, and take them smiling; if a fellow lost his temper at it everybody would laugh at him.

In jiu-jitsu they learn how to exercise and develop their muscles, how to catch hold of any enemy in many different ways so as to overpower him, how to throw him, and, what is very important, how to fall easily if they get thrown themselves.

Robert Baden-Powell,
***Boy Scouts Beyond the Seas: My World Tour*, 1913**

Baden-Powell's age when he was made Major General after his heroism at the Siege of Mafeking; he was the youngest to hold the rank at that time

IN B-P'S SHOES

People who have played Baden-Powell in TV, film and radio dramas:

Actor	Programme
Ian McKellen	*Be Prepared* (a radio drama, aired on Radio 4, 2004)
Basil Howes	*Juliette Low and the Girl Scouts* (TV, 1952)
Jasper Jacob	*The Edwardians* (TV, 1972)
Ron Moody	*The Edwardians* (TV, 1972)
David Niven (almost)	Shortly before his death in 1959, Cecil B DeMille started pre-production on a film biography of Baden-Powell's life and was in negotiations with David Niven to star in the film. It was never made.

DEAR BADEN-POWELL...

Even as early as 1908, Baden-Powell recognised the potential power of the problem page and set about answering his fellow Scouts' questions with suitable aplomb.

Dyeing Young

John, of Kent, is not content with the hair kindly nature had provided him with, and asks me for a good permanent dye. He goes on to tell me that his hair is of such a pronounced shade of red as to make him a conspicuous mark for the ill-natured remarks of his companions. I think if I were you, John, I would let well alone and let nature have her own way with you. Besides, there is no such thing as a permanent hair-dye, and you would have to dye your hair very frequently, or you would have periods of pie-baldness. As for the remarks of your boy friends, I don't think I would mind them. I am sure of one thing, your friends are not Scouts, or they would be more chary of hurting your feelings. At any rate, I would strongly advise you to put up with the colour of your hair, and by no means to do such a foolish thing as to dye it. Besides, however carefully you may dye your hair, it can be detected on close inspection, and I think remarks you would get about your dyed head would be more painful to bear than those you have put up with now. I may tell you that a few years ago there was a craze for red hair, and fashionable people went to the trouble of dyeing their hair to the required hue. Cheer up, John, the fashion may come in again. And red hair is as good as any other shade, anyhow.

'Round the Campfire'
in *The Scout*, No 1, Volume I,
18 April 1908

 Year in the twentieth century in which the film Henry Aldrich, Boy Scout *had its premier*

BE PREPARED (IN 32 DIFFERENT LANGUAGES)

1. Armenian – *misht badrast*
2. Belarusian – *napagatovye*
3. Croatian – *budi pripraven*
4. Danish – *vær forberedt*
5. Dutch – *weest paraat* or *wees bereid*
6. English – *be prepared*
7. Esperanto – *estu preta*
8. Estonian – *ole valmis*
9. Filipino – *laging handâ*
10. Finnish – *ole valmis*
11. French– *sois prêt* or *toujours prêt*
12. German – *allzeit bereit*
13. Hungarian – *légy résen*
14. Irish – *bí ullamh*
15. Italian – *sii preparato*
16. Japanese – *sonae-yo tsuneni*
17. Latin – *estote parati*
18. Latvian – *esi modrs*
19. Lithuanian – *budek*
20. Macedonian – *budi spreman*
21. Malay – *selalu bersedia*
22. Maltese – *kun lest*
23. Mongol – *belen bol*
24. Norwegian – *alltid beredt*
25. Persian – *aamaadeh baash*
26. Polish – *czuwaj*
27. Portuguese – *sempre alerta*
28. Serbian – *budi spreman*
29. Slovenian – *bodi pripravljen* or *bud pripavany*
30. Spanish – *siempre listo* or *siempre alerta*
31. Swedish – *var redo*
32. Ukrainian – *hotuis*

ONE MAN AND HIS BOAT

'Paddle your own canoe' was one of Baden-Powell's favourite mottos and even inspired the title and content of a whole book full of motivating yarns. It certainly triggered an idea for ex-Scout and brave oarsman Rob Munslow, who decided to cross the North Atlantic in a challenging solo row. He set off from Newfoundland, Canada, and after a gruelling 65 days, made it to his final destination across the ocean. For his efforts he became the world record holder for such a row and scored another entry into the *Guinness Book of Records* for the Scouts. His father believes his taste for adventure stems from his time in the Scouts.

DUNCAN DARES...
THE CURRENT CHIEF SCOUT

Some things you may or may not know about the UK's current Chief Scout, Peter Duncan...

- Born in London, 3 May 1954, Peter worked as an actor from the age of 15. He joined the National Theatre at 17, made several films including *Stardust* and *The Old Curiosity Shop*, and appeared in many TV series including *King Cinder*, *Sons and Lovers* and *Space: 1999*.
- Some may remember him as 'Young Treeman', a character that met with a grisly death in the 1980 film *Flash Gordon*. In the film, his hand was bitten off by an alien critter.
- Peter presented the children's TV show *Blue Peter* between September 1980 and November 1986, with a three-month break in the summer of 1984. His co-presenters were Simon Groom, Sarah Greene, Janet Ellis and Mark Curry. He soon became the 'action man' of the team.
- Peter's most famous feat on *Blue Peter* was running his first ever London marathon in 1981 and completing the Royal Marines' Endurance Course. He also cleaned the face of Big Ben – once a Scout, always a Scout.
- During his stint at *Blue Peter*, the production office received a number of complaints from parents about his scruffy image. In response, a 'design Peter an outfit' competition was launched. A green-and-white checked suit was declared the winner, and in many people's eyes, Peter has worn nothing else since.
- In June 1984 Peter left to film *Duncan Dares*, a full-time series of daring feats. On his last show he was also given the alien that had attacked him in *Flash Gordon* and reacquainted with Goldie, the *Blue Peter* dog.
- After *Blue Peter*, the other Peter – a man of many talents – found himself treading the boards in musicals *Barnum* and *Me and My Girl*. In 1995 he was nominated for an Olivier award as best actor for his role in the musical *The Card*. He also has his own production company and produced a stage version of *Erik the Viking* in 1993.
- Peter also found time to marry his partner Annie and have four children along the way. Together they went backpacking around the world in the TV travel documentaries *Travel Bug* and *Chinese Breakaway*.
- In 2004, he was made Chief Scout of the UK's half a million Scouts, at the rather sprightly age of 50. Traditionally, Chief Scouts have come from a military or civil service background. They also usually had experience as a Scout or Scout Leader. Peter had been a Wolf Cub, but his inception to the role was rather more about breaking the mould. As one Scout told the BBC: 'It's great to have a real action man as our Chief Scout.' A man after his own heart, B-P would surely agree.

 Percentage of people in the UK who recognised the Scout motto 'Be prepared' in a 2003 poll

SCOUTS ON THE SHELF

Three titles taking Scouting into the realm of modern literature (not all may be dressed in shorts):

The Radioactive Boy Scout: The Frightening True Story of a Whiz Kid and His Homemade Nuclear Reactor
by Ken Silverstein

Scout, the Christmas Dog
by Andrew Sansom and Clemente Guzman

A Boy Scout in Hollywood
by Brian J Hayes

Scouts in Bondage: And Other Books from an Innocent Age
edited by Michael Bell

NIGHTS AWAY

'I'm sorry Wilkinson, but there isn't a Beatnik Badge.'

Year in the twentieth century in which Austrian Boy Scouts are saluted at the 6th World Scout Jamboree in France; they had no presence under Hitler's rule

THE SCOUT PROMISE

The standard UK Scout Promise* is:

On my honour, I promise that I will do my best
to do my duty to God and to the Queen,
to help other people,
and to keep the Scout Law.

* There are now some available variations to accommodate different nationalities, religions and beliefs.

CELEBRITY SCOUTS: HARRISON FORD

What this famous Scout did next...

'Harrison Ford, the all-action hero' is a title he well deserves, both on and off screen. Known to millions as Han Solo, in the first *Star Wars* trilogy, and Indiana Jones – raider of the lost Arc and he of the Temple of Doom – it's hard to believe that one of the world's most coveted actors once found it hard to find work. He moved to California from Illinois in 1964 to find acting work but had little or no success at first. Thankfully, this actor was also a practical man and undertook some carpentry work between auditions. But in 1973 he got a small role in *American Graffiti* and his Black and Decker could finally take a back seat. As Indiana Jones he not only found his most memorable role, but also a common denominator in the Scouts. Both Harrison and 'Indy' were Scouts as boys. Harrison is reported to have undertaken the position of Scout camp meteorologist, while the character of Indy first appears as a Life Scout of the Boy Scouts of America in the opening of *Indiana Jones and the Last Crusade*. It is here that Indy first learns to use a bullwhip and receives his trademark fedora and chin scar while attempting to do a Scout good turn and secure the Cross of Coronado from thieves. In 2001, the real Harrison put his all-action hero status to real-life use and demonstrated his aerial bravery while rescuing a real Boy Scout lost on Table Mountain, Yellowstone National Park. On picking 13-year-old Cody Clawson up in his search and rescue helicopter, Harrison also displayed some of his on-screen charm with the words: 'Boy, you sure must have earned a merit badge for this one.' Apparently the boy had been dressed only in T-shirt and shorts and had survived a rainy night by taking cover under a rocky outcrop.

 Year in the twentieth century in which the 5th edition of Boy Scouts of America Handbook for Boys *was published*

READY TO RECEIVE!

Radio procedure signs as illustrated in *Handbook for Boys*, produced by the Boy Scouts of America, 1950

'Attention'	I have a message for you; make ready to receive.
'Go ahead'	I am ready to receive.
'Wait'	Wait – I will be ready to receive your or to finish in a moment.
'I cannot receive you'	Your signals are too weak.
'Break'	Beginning of text of message.
'End of word'	End of word.
'End of sentence'	Period.
'Error'	I have made a mistake and will repeat.
'Word received'	Made by receiver after each word to indicate received.
'Repeat'	Repeat.
'Message received'	Message is received completely.
'End of message'	Signing off – no more traffic.

SCOUTS UNITED

Look hard at the three words below.
Can you find the missing link?

- Aiming Off
- Bearing
- Thumbing

Answer on page 153.

CARTOON CAPERS: THE FLINTSTONES

Seems the Scouts have had something to get animated about for nearly 70 years. In the 1960s Scouts found their way into *The Flintstones*:

***The Flintstones*: 'Cave Scout Jamboree' (1964)**
The sudden accidental flooding of the gravel pit forces former Scoutmaster Fred to take a camping vacation with Barney, where he comes face to face with a huge Scout Jamboree.

***The Flintstones*: 'The Good Scout' (1961)**
Barney and Fred put bowling to one side and volunteer as Scoutmasters of 'the Sabertooth Tiger Patrol' instead.

AROUND THE WORLD IN 80 HOURS

Never mind *Around the World in 80 Days*, in 2006, former Scout – and indeed former member of the National Executive Board of Boy Scouts of America, Distinguished Eagle Scout and holder of the Silver Buffalo Award – Steve Fossett, set off on an epic journey.

The challenge he and partner Sir Richard Branson, another former Scout, had set themselves was to gain a world record for flying around the globe in under 80 hours. Steve took off in the specially built Virgin Atlantic GlobalFlyer on 28 February, watched by 8,000 people from the side of the runway in Salina, Kansas. His route was to take him over major cities including Montreal, London, Paris, Rome, Cairo, Bahrain, Karachi, Calcutta, Shanghai, Tokyo, Honolulu and Los Angeles.

Little more than three days later – 76 hours and 45 minutes to be precise – he had almost completed the circumnavigation and was heading for Kent where he was supposed to land. But while most of the journey had run quite smoothly (if you discount a challenging take-off, severe turbulence over India and constant concerns over the weakness of jet streams due to less than favourable weather patterns along the way), there was still some excitement to come. Steve had to make a dramatic emergency landing at Bournemouth Airport and drive to Kent International Airport in his own Citation X instead. The GlobalFlyer had experienced a large scale electrical malfunction just as Steve was preparing for his 40,000ft descent. He also only had 200lb of fuel left and a lack of visibility due to ice on the cockpit window.

True to his Scout skills, Steve called 'Mayday', observed the fifth Law of 'A Scout has courage in all difficulties' and after rerouting the plane virtually blind, finally hit ground bursting two tyres along the way. He made it back in one piece, thankfully, and proudly collected his world record for the 'longest non-stop flight'. This was also a relief for Sir Richard, who had still not made it around the world in his hot-air balloon despite several attempts between 1995 and 1998. He deemed fellow adventurer, Steve, 'a remarkable man'. A look at his website www.stevefossett.com and you can't argue with that.

QUOTE UNQUOTE

Wake up! Get busy! You only have the one life-day to live, so make the best of every minute of it.
Robert Baden-Powell on 'The Joy of the Open Road' in *Rovering to Success: A Book of Life-Sport for Young Men*, 1930

 Number of pence piece that commemorates the Centenary of Scouting

AN A-Z OF ACTIVITY BADGES: C-D

This most up-to-date list of Scout Activity Badges proves there's more than one reason to join the Scouts. The list is provided in bite-sized pieces throughout the book so as not to get badge addicts too over-excited.

- Camp Cook
- Camper
- Campsite Service
- Canoeist
- Caver
- Chef
- Circus Skills
- Climber
- Communicator
- Craft
- Cyclist
- Dinghy Sailor
- DIY
- Dragon Boating

CRACK THE CODE

Can you work out the Morse code message below, without cheating by using the reference on page 39?

.--- .- -- -... --- .-. . .

Clue: Sounds kinda fruity.

Answer on page 153.

NOTES FROM THE FOUNDER

B-P on uniform...

The Scout uniform, moreover, is simple and hygienic (a step now much in fashion) approximating that of our ancestors. Of this we are reminded when we sing round the campfire, to the tune of 'Men of Harlech'.

What's the good of wearing braces,
Vests and pants and boots with laces,
Spats, or hats you buy in places
Down in Brompton Road?

What's the use of shirts of cotton,
Studs that always get forgotten?
These affairs are simply rotten,
Better far is woad.

Robert Baden-Powell,
***Lessons from the Varsity of Life*, 1933**

CLEVER TO BE A CUB

Being a Cub Scout might look easy. But could you pass the First Star Test (as worn on the front of caps), dating back to 1916?

Before being awarded his first star a Tenderpad must:

a) Know the composition of the Union Flag and the right way to fly it.
b) Be able to tie the following knots, and know the uses – reef knot, sheet bend, clove hitch and fisherman's knot.
c) Turn a somersault; leap-frog over another boy the same size; bowl a hoop, or hop around a figure of eight course. Throw a ball, first with the right hand, then with the left, so that a boy 15 yards away catches it four times out of six.
d) Perform the first two body movements of the Scouts' physical exercises by himself, and know what their object is.
e) Know how and why he should keep his nails clean and cut, and his teeth clean; and why he should breathe through his nose.
f) Have at least three months' service as a Wolf Cub.

CELEBRITY SCOUTS: STEVEN SPIELBERG

What this famous Scout did next...

Perhaps the most celebrated of American Boy Scouts, Steven Spielberg not only ranks as one of the most influential film-makers in history, but was also personally responsible for the establishment of the Boy Scouts of America Cinematography Merit Badge in 1989. First nominated as 'family film-maker' while growing up in Phoenix, Arizona (his dad wasn't too handy with a camera), Spielberg honed his skills in the Boy Scouts, shooting a three-minute movie called *Gunsmorg* to earn his merit badge in photography. He used his fellow Scouts as actors and even faked a 'bad guy' falling off a cliff.

A proud recipient of the Distinguished Eagle Scout Award pre-fame, Spielberg never forgot his roots and somehow also managed to find time to act for a time on the board of the Boy Scouts of America (BSA). His Scouting enthusiasm lives on through the Cinematography Merit Badge. In order to receive this badge, Scouts have to display a host of film skills including displaying the 180-degree axis rule, preparing a storyboard for a movie feature, explaining what a 'gaffer' is, and shooting a vignette that could be used to train a new Scout in a Scouting skill.

Since those heady and experimental first days, he has gone on to win three Academy Awards, one for *Schindler's List* and another for *Saving Private Ryan*, and the Irving G Thalberg Memorial Award.

 Elevation to the nearest degree from the horizon to the Pole Star – something all Scouts should know

THINGS ALL SCOUTS SHOULD KNOW

In everyday life, both in town and country, there are interesting 'signs' to test your scoutcraft...
from *The Scout*, No 1, Volume I, 25 April 1908

How to hold an eel

If, during your visit to the seaside this year, you catch an eel, you will have some trouble in holding it unless you know the 'knack'. No difficulty will be experienced if you grasp it with index finger tucked under its belly (other fingers and thumb as you would normally wrap them around a pole), for by doing so the slippery customer is easily kept still, and the hook can be extracted.

DAH-DI-DAH-DI-DAH

How to punch numerals in Morse code, as explained in *Handbook for Boys*, produced by the Boy Scouts of America, 1950

1 di-dah-dah-dah-dah
2 di-di-dah-dah-dah
3 di-di-di-dah-dah
4 di-di-di-di-dah
5 di-di-di-di-dit
6 dah-di-di-di-dit
7 dah-dah-di-di-dit
8 dah-dah-dah-di-dit
9 dah-dah-dah-dah-dit
0 dah-dah-dah-dah-dah

AN OLYMPIC EFFORT

In 2012, it will be 64 years since the last Olympics were held in London. The Scouts are already hyped up to help out at the next event, spurred on by the fact that they will be following in the footsteps of former Scouts who represented the Movement at the 1948 event. That year, 60 Scouts were asked to take part in the biggest sporting event of the world. It is believed that they came from Uxbridge and London and helped out with a number of activities including showing people to their seats, carrying name placards for the opening and closing ceremonies, relaying messages back and forth along the high scaffold deck, and releasing pigeons into the stadium. Members of the Stop the Pigeon Society are currently praying that this final good turn will not be repeated by Scouts at the next Olympics.

LOOK OUT, SCOUTS!

A composition by Scout fan Rudyard Kipling to help you on your merry, Scouting way. Published in the September 1909 issue of the *Headquarters Gazette*.

A Patrol Song

These are our regulations–
There's just one law for the Scout,
And the first and the last, and the present and the past,
And the future and the perfect is 'Look out!'
O, thou, and he, look out!
We, ye, and they, look out!
Though you didn't or you wouldn't,
Or you hadn't or you couldn't;
You jolly well must look out!

Look out when you start for the day
That your kit is packed to your mind,
With half of it left behind.
Look out that your laces are tight,
And your boots are easy and stout,
Or you'll end with a blister by night.
(Chorus) All patrols look out!

Look out for the birds of the air,
Look out for the beasts of the field;
They'll tell you how and where
The other side's concealed.
When the blackbird bolts from the copse,
And the cattle are staring about,
The wise commander stops
And (Chorus) All patrols look out!

Look out when your front is clear,
And you feel you are bound to win.
Look out for your flank and for your rear–
For that's when surprises begin.
For the rustle that isn't a rat,
For the splash that isn't a trout,
For the boulder that may be a hat,
(Chorus) All patrols look out!

For the innocent knee-high grass,
For the ditch that never tells.
Look out! Look out ere you pass–

54 *Number of countries in the Commonwealth – something all Scouts should know; member countries drawn largely from the former British Empire*

And look out for everything else!
A sign mid-read as you run
May turn retreat to a rout–
For all things under the sun,
(Chorus) All patrols look out!

Look out when your temper goes
At the end of the losing game;
And your boots are too tight for your toes,
And you answer, argue and blame.
But it has to be learned by the Scout–
For whining and shirking and 'jaw',
(Chorus) All patrols look out!

NIGHTS AWAY

The fire brigade was called on news of the mass rubbing-two-sticks-together-athon.

Year in the twentieth century of the 8th World Scout Jamboree held in Canada; the first major international Scout event held outside Europe

AN EXPLOSIVE SITUATION

All Scouts are urged to 'be prepared' but Birmingham's 2nd Wylde Green Scout Group and their Leader came up against an explosive situation in early 2006. Out and about on an unsuspecting hike in local Sutton Park they found a grenade in the mud that could detonate at any time. Leader Mile Westley quickly moved his Troop to a safe distance away before gently moving the hand grenade out of harm's way (a very brave move!). He then alerted park rangers who called in the bomb squad, which carried out a controlled explosion that thankfully did not harm any of the surrounding area, wildlife or visitors to the park. It is believed that the grenade dated back more than 60 years, when the Home Guard carried out training exercises in the area. A pity they didn't also exercise the sixth Scout Law to '...be careful of possessions and property'.

GET READY FOR THE GANG SHOW

Ten effective little Scout plays from *The Scout*, 27 October 1949, apparently each 'taking no more than 15 or 20 minutes to perform':

1. *The Boy Who Came Too Late*
2. *Blue Ray*
3. *Any More for the Skylark?*
4. *Variations on a Camp Theme*
5. *SOS*
6. *West of the Khyber*
7. *One Minute to Spare!*
8. *The Operative Hike and Big Bad Wolf*
9. *Dobbin Does it Again*
10. *Adventus*

QUOTE UNQUOTE

Girl Scout: Is this made from real lemons?
Wednesday: Yes.
Girl Scout: I only like all-natural foods and beverages, organically grown, with no preservatives. Are you sure they're real lemons?
Pugsley: Yes.
Girl Scout: I'll tell you what. I'll buy a cup if you buy a box of my delicious Girl Scout cookies. Do we have a deal?
Wednesday: Are they made from real Girl Scouts?

From the film *The Addams Family*, 1991

 Number of moons that the planet Saturn is thought to have – another thing all Scouts should know, especially those who want their Astronomer's Badge

PROVE YOUR PROFICIENCY

Bagging a Boy Scout's Proficiency Badge circa 1909 could be harder than you think.

To wear a **Master-at-Arms** Badge, you must be able to...
Gain proficiency in two of the following subjects:
single-stick
quarter-staff
fencing
boxing
jiu-jitsu
and wrestling.

LAYING DOWN THE LAW

The Law of the Jungle lays down very clearly that any wolf may, when he marries, withdraw from the Pack he belongs to; but as soon as his cubs are old enough to stand on their feet he must bring them to the Pack Council, which is generally held once a month at full moon, in order that the other wolves may identify them...

...Father Wolf waited till his cubs could run a little, and then on the night of the Pack Meeting took them and Mowgli and Mother Wolf to the Council Rock -- a hilltop covered with stones and boulders where a hundred wolves could hide. Akela, the great gray Lone Wolf, who led all the Pack by strength and cunning, lay out at full length on his rock, and below him sat forty or more wolves of every size and colour, from badger-coloured veterans who could handle a buck alone, to young black three-year-olds who thought they could. The Lone Wolf had led them for a year now. He had fallen twice into a wolf-trap in his youth, and once he had been beaten and left for dead; so he knew the manners and customs of men. There was very little talking at the Rock. The cubs tumbled over each other in the centre of the circle where their mothers and fathers sat, and now and again a senior wolf would go quietly up to a cub, look at him carefully, and return to his place on noiseless feet. Sometimes a mother would push her cub far out into the moonlight, to be sure that he had not been overlooked. Akela from his rock would cry: '*Ye know the Law -- ye know the Law. Look well, O Wolves!*' and the anxious mothers would take up the call: '*Look -- look well, O Wolves!*'

Rudyard Kipling,
***The Jungle Book*, 1894.**
The characters described largely inspired Baden-Powell's Wolf Cubs, including the Law.

THE CAMP COOK: BURGERS IN LEAVES

From *Backwoods Cooking – Practical Methods and Recipes*, a reprint of a popular collection that first appeared in *Scouting* magazine.

You will need:

- Cabbages
- Beefburgers or mince

Method:

1. Place three layers of cabbage leaves directly onto the hot embers and put the beefburgers or mince patties on top of them.
2. After approximately 10 minutes, turn the meat over, putting on to three new cabbage leaves. Repeat this process until the meat is cooked.

Notes:

Cabbage leaves can replace silver foil in many instances when using backwoods cooking recipes. It is important that on no occasion should rhubarb leaves be used, as these contain a highly poisonous resin.

'CARROTS', A TRUE SCOUT

'Carrots' was a red-haired boy who lived at one time in Shoreditch. He earned a precious living selling papers. His mother – more often drunk than sober – beat the poor kid when he had not sufficient pennies. At last she drove him from the hovel he called home and he took to sleeping rough near Leadenhall Market.

As an article in *The Scouter*, March 1930 went on to explain, Carrots begged to be taken in by Dr Barnado's Homes but there was no room until the following week. When the man from the home went back, Carrots wasn't there. He had died from starvation, and was found in such a state in a barrel just that morning having crawled in to try and get some sleep. The boy he was with survived.

On quizzing Carrot's fellow urchin friends it turned out that he had spent his last two coppers on some faggots (strips of cheap meat) that he didn't keep for himself but shared among his friends. Unfortunately, his own portion was not enough to sustain his weakened body.

It was 'this kind of boy, so noisy, so dirty, and to some people so unattractive, yet often with such strains of splendour' that was used by the author as an example of how a Scout should be – one who remembers that there is no greater love than the love of him who lays down his life for his friends.

 Number on the periodic table of Cerium, similar to iron and the most common 'rare' earth element on the planet – something all Scouts should know

YOU'LL BE A SCOUT, MY SON...

If you can 'freeze' without a sign of fear
When crusty rhinos come galumphing near,
Or face an elephant whose ears and trunk
Would put most people in an awful funk;
If you can keep your temper and can laugh
When bullies rile you with insulting chaff;
If you can keep our law through thick and thin
When others tempt you in the ways of sin;
If you can stand when men in panic run
You'll be a Scout, what's more, a MAN, my son.

A parody of Rudyard Kipling's 'If', published by Robert Baden-Powell in *Paddle Your Own Canoe or Tips For Boys – From The Jungle and Elsewhere,* 1939. It is not known if B-P got Rudyard's permission first.

QUOTE UNQUOTE

Doctors will prescribe early-rising, plain food, moderate exercise, and all that kind of thing, but give me laughter, and plenty of it.
Robert Baden-Powell,
Life's Snags and How to Meet Them, 1936

WHOSE BADGE IS IT ANYWAY?

You might have a full arm of new badges. Or you may be taking a trip down memory lane. But can you guess what this Cub Scout Proficiency Badge is for?

a) S-winger
b) Air-spotter
c) Pigeon-carrier

Answer on page 153.

Number of Scout stamps issued in 1957, the 50th anniversary of Scouting, according to www.sossi.org, the Scouts on Stamps Society International

SOMETHING ABOUT BROWNSEA

Fifteen facts about Brownsea, location of the first experimental Scout camp, that you may not otherwise have the good fortune to know:

One
It was chosen as the location for Baden-Powell's experimental Scout camp in 1907.

Two
It has survived Viking invasion, marauding pirates and the Spanish Armada.

Three
It was a popular haunt of the European nobility in the early nineteenth century.

Four
It was a favourite of the Prince Regent who had no idea there could be 'such a delightful spot in the Kingdom'.

Five
Peacocks and Sika deer roam free there.

Six
It supports one of Britain's last remaining colonies of red squirrels.

Seven
It is home to an 'Explorer's Trail', a 'Smuggler's Trail' and a 'Historical Trail' as maintained by the National Trust.

Eight
It has its own church, built in 1854 by the island's owner, Colonel William Petrie Waugh.

Nine
A chapel established here by the monks of nearby Cerne Abbey was sacked by King Canute and a party of Vikings in 1015.

Ten
The John Lewis Partnership use Brownsea Castle as a country club and hotel.

Eleven
Brownsea Castle was built by King Henry VIII as part of a move to fortify the South Coast against invaders.

Twelve
A French pirate ship crashed here in 1574.

Thirteen
Colonel Waugh bought the island in 1854 believing it to be rich in clay suitable for fine porcelain – unfortunately he was incorrect.

Fourteen
Mrs Mary Bonham-Christie, the last of Brownsea's owners, was an eccentric recluse who determined that the island should be returned to nature.

Fifteen
Following Mrs Bonham-Christie's back to wilderness bid, Brownsea was known as the 'Secret Island' to the people of nearby Poole.

 Number in thousands of Scouts awarded the National Service Badge for their hard work during World War II

AN A-Z OF ACTIVITY BADGES: E-H

This most up-to-date list of Scout Activity Badges proves there's more than one reason to join the Scouts. The list is provided in bite-sized pieces throughout the book so as not to get badge addicts too over-excited.

- Electronics
- Emergency Aid (5 stages)
- Entertainer
- Equestrian
- Fire Safety
- Forester
- Global Conservation
- Guide
- Heritage
- Hiker
- Hike's Away (staged)
- Hill Walker
- Hobbies

QUOTE UNQUOTE

There is no pleasure that comes near to that of preparing your own meal over your little fire of wood embers at the end of the day, and no scent like the smell of that fire.
Robert Baden-Powell on 'The joy of the open road' in *Rovering to Success: A Book of Life-Sport for Young Men,* 1930

LOST TO THE SKIFFLE

A story of one Scout who got lost along the way, as told by Hazel Addis in *The Scouter*, 1960.

Marigold was 16 when she became a Scout. She had never been a Guide, but remarked naively that she thought she was good with boys. She was. She was friends with one of the seniors and thought she would like to join the same Movement.

So, at 16, she took the Scout Promise and donned a CI Badge. And at 16 she had grown tired of her seniors and of Cubbing. She just faded away, without remembering to explain to Akela, and joined a skiffle group instead.

Well, if you can't be a butterfly at 16, when can you? But we like the new rule that would-be girl CIs must obtain the consent of the ADC (assistant district commissioner) (Cubs) and the GSM (group Scout master) before they start their probation. And before they take the Promise the DC (district commissioner) or ADC (Cubs) and GSM, as well as the CM (county manager) must be satisfied that they mean to kept it – and not flutter by.

KEY SCOUTING DATES: 1940s

1941

January Baden-Powell dies at Paxtu, Nyeri, Kenya. A memorial service is held at Westminster Abbey and Lord Somers is appointed Chief Scout in his place.

1945

May Germany agrees unconditional surrender and World War II ends. Gilwell Park reopens and, during the course of the year, 12,000 Scouts camp there.

1946

August An organisation for British Scouts in Germany is established.

1948

May-June The first post-war production of *Boy Scout* takes place at the Royal Albert Hall, London (it was staged again in 1949, 1951, 1953, 1955 and 1959).

1949

April First 'Bob-a-Job' week.

CELEBRITY SCOUTS: RAY MEARS

What this famous Scout did next...

Hands-on, practical action, out in the bush is what Ray Mears does best. Ever since his judo teacher Kingsley declared: 'You don't need equipment, you need knowledge to survive in the wild,' Ray has been taking the Robinson Crusoe approach. And with his very own School of Wilderness Bushcraft (Woodlore) and several TV series and books under his belt (*Tracks*, *World of Survival* and *Extreme Survival* among others) his leadership in the field looks set to survive. Staying true to the appeal and importance of Scouting skills in everyday life, Mears waxes lyrical about the merits of *Scouting for Boys*: 'It's a book we recommend to clients taking survival courses as it contains hundreds of practical tips still useful today. In some parts, it's certainly a book of its time, but much of B-P's rough guide to the outdoors still stands us in good stead.' Through the 'Scouts Go Green' initiative he has also helped to promote awareness of environmental issues among young people where participating Scouts can earn the new Environment Group Award. Ray also champions the lost art of tracking: 'You, too, could watch a woodmouse clean his whiskers, an adder bathe in the dappled woodland light, a badger cleaning out his den,' his website declares.

 Year in the twentieth century in which the film To Kill a Mockingbird *was premiered starring Mary Badham as Scout*

CARTOON CAPERS: THE SIMPSONS

Seems the Scouts have had something to get animated about for nearly 70 years. In the 1990s, the Scouts made their way into The Simpsons...

***The Simpsons*: 'Boy Scoutz 'n' the Hood' (1993)**

Bart joins the Junior Campers Scout organisation where he has a series of misadventures.

***The Simpsons*: 'Bart of War' (2003)**

Bart joins the Pre-Teen Braves while Milhouse joins the Calvary Kids. It's Scout Patrol war!

EQUAL EFFORTS FOR THE WAR

B-P was determined that Scouting should be for everyone, of all abilities, colours and creeds. An article in *The Scouter*, January 1940, described how 'handicapped Scouts' could help in Air Raid Precautions (ARP) and contribute to the war effort:

- By passing their Ambulance badge.
- By passing their Firearm badge when possible.
- By learning elementary ARP, and knowing what to do.
- By learning self-control, and how to give help and courage to those weaker than themselves.
- By learning how to give and remember messages. This can be practiced as a patrol game.
- By learning how to use a telephone, if possible.
- By learning how to send messages and warning in the Morse code by buzzer or whistle.
- By knowing how to assemble the civilian mask, and how to fit other people correctly. Also how to assemble the respirator boxes.
- Be able to make dark shapes for lamps.
- Be able to make and fill sandbags as required.
- Be able to act as clerks and messengers to Air Raid Wardens in their own hospital or institution.
- Know the dangers of panic, and be able and responsible to conduct people to Air Raid Shelters.
- Understand something about the making of Air Raid Shelters, and if able, have helped to make one.
- Turn all this useful Scout knowledge to good account should any emergency arise, and BE PREPARED now.

Year in the twentieth century in which the 11th World Scout Jamboree was held in Greece; this was the scene of the biggest Scout airlift at the time

QUOTE UNQUOTE

The guys who wrote this cartoon don't know squat. Itchy should have tied Scratchy's tongue with a taut-line hitch, not a sheet bend.
Bart Simpson (after Itchy makes Scratchy into a tent) in the 'Boy-Scoutz 'n' the Hood' episode of *The Simpsons*

READY, STEADY, SCOUT: PART II

Contrary to popular belief, the Scouts was not established as an 'organisation' but rather more organic in its spread, picking up legions of fans along the way. The first Scout census of 1910 would count a phenomenal 100,000 members. Here, Baden-Powell tells his own account of how it all began, in 'How I started Scouting', *The Scout*, No 1, Volume I, 18 April 1908...

I remember how in our sailing-boat we ran on some rocks one day in rather a nasty little sea, and, as the boat heeled over and rolled about, I thought all was up with us; and I huddled down helplessly, waiting to see what was to happen.

I was quite prepared, like the frog in the milk, to give up all efforts to save myself.

Story of a boathook

Just then a boathook which had become dislodged slipped and fell overboard into the sea, and I was thinking how soon I was probably to follow it when I was suddenly recalled to life by a string of remarks from my eldest brother, who was in command, abusing me for sitting by and letting the boathook go overboard and telling me to grab hold of it before it floated out of reach, which I quickly did.

I then saw that if he was so mighty particular about saving an old boathook at that juncture there might be some hope for our saving ourselves. So I bucked up and set to work to help the others. In the end we got off safe and sound. But that lesson of the boathook has been of the greatest use to me many a time since in tight places when things were looking very bad. I have remembered that then was the time to wake up and work extra hard and not to give in, and if people round-about were looking glum and nervous, the thing was to suggest some small thing to think about and to carry out to remind them that matters were not so hopeless after all.

For instance, in the case of an unpleasantly strong attack by the enemy, when some people were beginning to think that things looked bad for us, it came in useful to sing out: 'Where's the cook? Isn't it about time we had breakfast?' and that seemed to set them all right again and to give them heart to carry on.

 Year in the twentieth century when British Scouts visited Japan for the first time

NIGHTS AWAY

Joe hadn't seen a girl for a while and wanted to get it all on tape.

SCOUTING SONGSTERS

David Bowie • Norman Cook, aka Fat Boy Slim
Jarvis Cocker • Mark Feehily
Boy George • David Gilmour
Simon Mayo • Sir Paul McCartney
George Michael • Finley Quaye
Sir Cliff Richard • Ian Wallace
Pete Waterman • Steve Wright

Door number – from 65-67 Queen's Gate, London SW7 – of Baden-Powell House Activity Centre offering accommodation and activities for Scouts

PROVE YOUR PROFICIENCY

Bagging a Boy Scout's Proficiency Badge circa 1909 could be harder than you think.

To wear a **Handyman** Badge, you must be able to...

- Paint a door or bath
- Whitewash a ceiling
- Repair gas fittings, tap-washers, sash lines, window and door fittings
- Replace gas mantles and electric light bulbs
- Hang pictures and curtains
- Repair blinds
- Fix curtains and portiere rods, bind fixtures, lay carpets, mend clothing and upholstery
- Do small furniture and china repairs
- Sharpen knives

CELEBRITY SCOUTS: VAL DOONICAN

What this famous Scout did next...

Born Michael Valentine Doonican on 3 February 1927, the 'man with a girl's name' was a household legend of the 1970s on TV programmes such as *Val Doonican's Music Show*. The undisputed king of the rocking chair wooed fans with his velvet crooning, laid-back guitar and creative array of cardigans – but it wasn't always so. According to Val himself he was 'an overnight success after 17 years' and since leaving school at 14 years it took much touring and hard work before he found his place in 'the chair'. But as one of eight children, who often found they had to forage for food, hard work was never a problem. His career began at Scouts where he found a platform on which to perform. As portrayed in *Scouting* magazine, March 1990, Val was 'much involved with our campfire entertainment, playing mandolin duets with a cousin of mine and running my first vocal quartet.' Val was also a member of the Troop's pipe playing band (on side drum, tenor drum and bass drum). Such piping bands had become something of a Scout tradition by the 1960s, and in 1969, one made its television debut when it played on the programme *This is Your Life*. The episode was in honour of none other than Val, of course. The champion of such hits as 'Quit Kickin' My Dog Around' could have let his success go to his head but a humble Scout attitude saved him. After 50 hit albums, he now performs the odd regional show (much to the delight of hardcore fans) but prefers to spend the rest of his time in the countryside.

 Year in the twentieth century in which Pink Floyd – former Scouts David Gilmour and Syd Barrett – brought psychedelia to London at the Roundhouse

THE WHISTLING SONG

'The Whistling Song' was just one of B-P's rousing compositions, published in the July 1909 to December 1910 issue of *Headquarters Gazette*, emphasising the doctrine that: 'A Scout smiles and whistles under all circumstances' and 'every patrol in the kingdom should know and use it long before the year is out.' Verses can be changed to suit your activities...

When fun's about the Scouts are out.
And out upon the trail,
And each Patrol seeks out its goal
By road, or river, or rail.
Hoh!

Old Tommy Smooks wears saucy boots,
When out upon the trail,
And each Patrol seeks out its goal
By road, or river, or rail.
Hoh!

And Willy Jones will rattle his bones.
When out upon the trail,
Etc.

It's 'be prepareds', and don't be scared
By difficult work or play,
To play the fife, or save a life,
Is all in the work of the day.
Hoh!

MERITS OF A GIRL GUIDE

Girl Guide skills required, as described in the *Headquarters Gazette*, November 1909

2nd-CLASS GUIDE

Badge – motto, 'be prepared', on left arm

As soon as a girl can pass tests in the knowledge of the rules of the corps; can lay and light a fire; make a bed, and cut out and sew a Union Jack.'

1st-CLASS GUIDE

Fleur-de-lys badge on left arm

One shilling in savings bank; cook a simple dish; know simple first aid bandaging; and know simple hospital nursing.

Year in the twentieth century in which the Disney film of Rudyard Kipling's The Jungle Book *premiered; the book that inspired Cub Scouting*

PATROL NAMES AND THEIR PECULIARITIES: THE OWL

As referred to in an enlightening series by JR Stanley (author of *Five Boys and a Master*) in *The Scouter*, January 1930:

- The official patrol flag of the Owl Patrol shows the long-eared owl.
- Owls are of great use to mankind and destroy multitudes of rats and mice, with an occasional bird to boot.
- Owls are easily recognized by their quaint half-human faces and feathered trousers.
- Owls do not trouble about an elaborate nest but choose a hole in the wall, a cliff, a tree, or inside a barn.
- Owls have a peculiar habit of rejecting the undigested parts of their food through the beak in the form of pellets (sometimes called squids).
- Owls usually hunt at night. An appearance of an owl by day is often the signal for a crowd of small birds to mob them.
- The eyes of an owl appear to be fixed like a doll's, but as the head works on a swivel all is well.
- An owl's pupils open widely at night to admit the faintest beams of light.
- The Owl Patrol call of 'Koot-koot-koo' can be imitated by blowing through cupped hands.
- The feathers of an owl are wonderfully soft, rendering their flight noiseless.
- Scouts who belong to the Owl Patrol should remember that: 'The wise old owl sat on an oak ; The more he thought, the less he spoke.'

THE SHORTER, BUT STILL GRAND HOWL

When the Wolf Cubs became the Cubs, the mysterious 'dybs' and 'dobs' were removed from the Grand Howl to leave the much shorter version below:

THE CUB HOWL

On the Leader's signal (raising and lowering arms), the Cubs squat down, hands between feet.
Cubs: Akela, we'll do our best.
Spring to feet.
Leading Cub: Salutes Cubs! Do your best.
Cubs: [salute] We will do our best.
And the Leader takes the salute.

 Number of countries represented at the Scout Eurojam held in Hylands Park, Essex in 2005

SCOUTING SKILLS: NAVIGATION

Scouting skills to help you survive the wild, by Sir Ranulph Fiennes from *100 Years of Scouting* DVD (Endemol, 2007)

1. The easiest way to navigate is look for obvious landmarks that you can also pinpoint on a map.
2. Make sure you have the right equipment and spares. Remember, your GPS might fail but a compass and map should always see you right.
3. An expedition should always have two or three good navigators on it, if possible. Always take a local guide if you can.

QUOTE UNQUOTE

...Across the river at the Pentagon sits an Eagle Scout from Illinois who Americans count on to 'be prepared'.
US President George W Bush
talking about secretary of defence Donald Rumsfeld, 2005

NOTES FROM THE FOUNDER

B-P on the Scout logo, the *fleur-de-lys*...

In the Middle Ages Charles, King of Naples, owing to his French descent had the fleur-de-lys as his crest. It was in his reign that Flavio Gioja, the navigator, made the mariners compass into a practical and reliable instrument. The compass card had the initial letters of North, South, East and West on it. In Italian the North was "Tramontana." So he put a capital T to mark the North point. But in compliment to the King he made a combination of the letter T with the King's fleur-de-lys crest. From that time the North point has been universally shown on the maps, charts, and compass cards by that sign. The actual meaning to be read from the fleur-de-lys badge is that it points in the right direction (and upwards) turning neither to the right nor left, since these lead backwards again. The stars on the two side arms stand for the two eyes of the Wolf Cub having been opened before he became a Scout, when he gained his First-Class Badge of two Stars. The three points represent the three elements of the Scout's Promise-Duty to God and King, Helpfulness to other people and the Obedience to the Scout Law.

Robert Baden-Powell,
***Lessons from the Varsity of Life*, 1933**

Year in the twentieth century in which former Scouts Neil Armstrong and Buzz Aldrin walked on the moon, after piloting the spacecraft Apollo 11

NIGHTS AWAY

That was the summer that the title of 'Chief Scout' went to B-P's head.

FIRST PATROL

Leaders who took charge of B-P's first nominated Patrols at Brownsea:

Wolves	Musgrave C (Bob) Wroughton
Bulls	Thomas Brian Evans-Lombe
Curlews	George Rodney
Ravens	Herbert Emley

 Number of countries represented at the 6th World Scout Jamboree – the 'Jamboree for Peace' – held in 1947 on the banks of the River Seine, France

Gilwell Park is a 108-acre site that now acts as both Scouting headquarters and a campsite for Scouts and their Leaders to use throughout the year. But it wasn't always so. Here are some of Gilwell's former owners:

The recorded history of Gilwell can be traced back to 1407 and was owned by a John Crow, where the land is listed under the name of Glydiefords.

Sometime between 1407 and 1422, Crow sold the land to Richard Rolfe, and the area became known as Gillrolfes – 'Gill' being the Old English for glen and 'Rolfe' the surname of the owner. Following Rolfe's death in 1422, different sections of the property came to be called 'Great Gilwell' and 'Little Gilwell' – 'wella' meaning spring.

Around 1422, a further 14 acres was acquired in the area by Richard Osbourne who then built a large dwelling on the site called Osbourne Hall. This stood for 300 years. Legend has it that, in the early 1500s, King Henry VIII owned the land and built a hunting lodge for his son Edward. However, there is no proof of this.

In 1736 the infamous highwayman Dick Turpin was said to have begun using Gilwell's forests to conceal himself from authorities and to ambush travellers and freight on their way to London. (Something he surely wouldn't have dared if the Scouts had been there.)

William Skrimshire purchased Great Gilwell, Little Gilwell, and half of Osborne's estate, including Osborne Hall in 1754. He demolished the old Osborne Hall and built a new residence. This building is now called the White House and is the basis of the UK's Scout Headquarters.

The estate was bought by Leonard Tresilian and then passed into the Chinnery family through the marriage of the eldest Tresilian daughter, Margaret, to William, the brother of the artist George Chinnery. During Chinnery's time, Gilwell was visited by King George III, the Prince Regent (later George IV) and Prince Adolphus (George III's seventh son).

In 1824, Gilwell was acquired by Thomas Usbourne. When the original London Bridge was replaced in 1826, he erected pieces of it behind the White House, on what is now the Buffalo Lawn.

William Gibbs, a poet and inventor, bought the estate in 1858 before William F de Bois Maclaren purchased it for the Scouts in 1919 for £7,000.

An official opening of the training and camp centre for Scouts was held on 26 July 1919. Baden-Powell never lived there but did take it as his territorial designation in his peerage title of Baron Baden-Powell of Gilwell, in 1929.

Year in the twentieth century in which Idi Amin led a military coup in Uganda, bringing Scouting there to a halt; it was rehabilitated in 1986

NOTES FROM THE FOUNDER

B-P on making men out of slobs...

That is what this book is for; to show how real men can be made out of slobs and how slobs can make themselves into men if they like to try.

What on earth is a 'slob', you may ask. Well – I don't know myself. The word doesn't come in any dictionary that I know of, but I take it to mean that a slob is a boy who is inclined to look on at games or work, rather than join in them himself, who likes to go to the 'flicks' (if other people pay for his seat) and who smokes cigarettes in the hope of looking manly when it only makes him look a young fool.

In other words, a slob is a young slacker. Yet a slacker who leads a miserable life, no good to himself or to anyone else, can if he likes, be turned into a hefty, happy and useful MAN.

Robert Baden-Powell, *Adventuring to Manhood*, 1936

CRACK THE CODE

Can you work out the Morse code message below, without cheating by using the reference on page 39?

- .... . / -... --- -.-- / ... -.-. --- ..- - ...

Clue: Fine name before the girls arrived.

Answer on page 153.

NAME THAT TUNE

Scouting songs, some of which may not be so suitable for around the campfire:

Gerry Rafferty .... *I Was a Boy Scout*
John Denver .... *Going Camping*
Naughty By Nature .... *Jamboree*
Ninjaman .... *Bad Boy Nuh Cub Scout*
Pink Squares .... *I Was a Boy Scout*
Scout Niblett .... *Kidnapped by Neptune*
Shithook .... *When a Boy Scout gets the Blues*
Tiger Tiger .... *Dream Scout*
Tom Lehrer .... *Be Prepared*

 Average number of heartbeats per minute of a resting adult – something all Scouts should know, especially those who want their First Aid Badge

MORE SCOUTS ON SCREEN

Just a few of the films that have featured Scouts in them:

Remise du drapeau aux boy-scouts au Cinquantenaire (1914)
The Little Boy Scout (1917)
Tex Rides with the Boy Scouts (1937)
Scouts to the Rescue (1939)
Room for One More (1952)
Scoutmaster Magoo (1958)
Sgt Pepper's Lonely Hearts Club Band (1978)
Scout's Honor (1980)
Star Trek II: The Wrath of Khan (1982)
The Wrong Guys (1988)
Troop Beverly Hills (1989)
The Last Boy Scout (1991) *
Scout's Honor (2001)
The Pacifier (2005)
Yours, Mine and Ours (2005)

* Actually, despite the title, this one doesn't actually include a Boy Scout at all... just Bruce Willis on the rampage.

A NEW DAWN FOR SCOUTING

On 1 August 2007, millions of Scouts and former Scouts from across the globe will take part in Scouting's Sunrise. This special date was set to celebrate the past, present and future of Scouting. It takes place exactly 100 years after Baden-Powell ran his experimental Scout Camp on Brownsea Island. As the sun rises across the world, Scouts will gather together in their millions to renew their Promise, do a good turn and present Gifts for Peace projects and celebrate with their communities.

At a unique event on Brownsea Island between 30 July and 1 August 2007, two Scouts each from more than 150 nations will gather to celebrate the sunrise. Participants will travel from the World Scout Jamboree at Hylands Park. They will then take part in a new time trail, visiting the 'continents' of the world and discovering their Scouting music, dance, food, culture and religion. This is followed by a 'world carnival'. Then, in the morning they will be woken to the sound of the African kudu horn that Baden-Powell used to wake his original camp. After a morning ceremony, the Scouts will enjoy a day of activities and then return to the Jamboree to join their fellow Scouts ready for the next 100 years.

ROVER TO YOU

Public opinion on *Rovering to Success: A Book of Life Sport for Young Men* by Robert Baden-Powell, 1930: some extracts from letters received by the author:

From a young man:

When I last saw my mother she said to me: 'Take *Rovering to Success* in place of advice from me. You cannot do better.'

From a Scoutmaster:

I have found it difficult to speak to my older boys on questions of manhood. Your book has solved the question for me and I am giving a copy to each of my older Scouts.

From a journalist:

Allow me to say I think your book the most efficacious tonic in the world of books today.

QUOTE UNQUOTE

Scouting has blazed a trail where others now follow.
Tony Blair, prime minister

THE WAY THAT YOU WOGGLE

When it comes to neck attire in the Scouts, it's not just about what you wear, but the way that you woggle...

The Scout scarf – or neckerchief as it was originally called – began its days loosely knotted at the neck. This meant that it became creased very easily where it was tied. To get around this, a few Scouts at Gilwell thought they'd begin experimenting with other ways to hold the two ends together. They had heard that the Americans had come up with the idea of using a ring or 'boon doogle' made from bone, rope or wood through which the ends could be pulled. When one of the Scouts began making a Turks Head knot (a decorative rope knot sometimes made at sea to pass the time), they knew they were on the right track. They made their knot out of thin sewing machine leather belting, and the woggle was born! Well almost, because then they had to come up with the name. Some say the word woggle comes from boon doogle. Others think it could be inspired by the sixteenth-century word 'waggle' meaning 'to move anything held or fixed at one end to or fro with quick short motions'. Either way it got its first fashion outing in *The Scout*, 9 June 1923, in an article entitled 'Wear a scarf woggle' and in *Scouting for Boys* the same year. And where some Scouts dared to woggle, others followed suit.

 Year in the twentieth century in which Ralph Reader presents the final London Gang Show, after deciding to retire at the age of 71 years

SCOUTING YARNS: THE WOLF PACK

Hunting song of the Seeonee pack...

As the dawn was breaking the Sambhur belled
Once, twice and again!
And a doe leaped up, and a doe leaped up
From the pond in the wood where the wild deer sup.
This I, scouting alone, beheld,
Once, twice and again!
As the dawn was breaking the Sambhur belled
Once, twice and again!
And a wolf stole back, and a wolf stole back
To carry the word to the waiting pack,
And we sought and we found and we bayed on his track
Once, twice and again!
As the dawn was breaking the Wolf-Pack yelled
Once, twice and again!
Feet in the jungle that leave no mark!
Eyes that can see in the dark – the dark!
Tongue – give tongue to it! Hark! O hark!
Once, twice and again!

Rudyard Kipling, *The Jungle Book*, 1894

GET TRACKING

Identifying animals by their tracks was a huge part of Scouting in B-P's time. Here are some tips for novice animal trackers today:

The badger
Look for five digits and a large kidney-shaped pad. Look nearby for coarse white-tipped hairs caught on fences and the bark of trees.

The otter
Another five-digit mammal with an almost round pad. In very soft soils you might see evidence of webbing between the digits.

The fox
A fox track is very dog-like, but far more compact. The print has four digits with the outer two curved towards the inner ones.

The deer
An easy one! The deer is cloven hoofed, with only two toe digits.

The rabbit
Look near burrows for the long exaggerated imprints of the hind legs.

Number of nights away Scouts are required to sleep – in tents, bivouacs, camps, hostels or boats – to gain the Nights Away 75 Staged Activity Badge 75

WHOSE BADGE IS IT ANYWAY?

You might have a full arm of new badges. Or you may be taking a trip down memory lane. But can you guess what this Cub Scout Proficiency Badge is for?

a) Bushman
b) Fire safety
c) Gardener

Answer on page 153.

WE ARE THE WORD

Ten words or phrases in the English language that will forever be connected with Scouts:

1. Badges
2. Beaver
3. Camp
4. Cub
5. Dyb-dyb-dyb
6. Jamboree
7. Gang Show
8. Rover
9. Scout
10. Woggle

QUOTE UNQUOTE

Bertie: What are you doing here?
Edwin: I'm tidying your room. It's my last Saturday's act of kindness.
Bertie: Last Saturday's?
Edwin: I'm five days behind. I was six till last night, but I polished your shoes.

Bertie Wooster to Edwin the Boy Scout in PG Wodehouse's *Carry on Jeeves*, 1925

 Year in the twentieth century that young ladies were allowed into the Venture Scouts

CELEBRITY SCOUTS: SIR RANULPH FIENNES

What this famous Scout did next...

Sir Ranulph Twisleton-Wykeham Fiennes, 3rd Baronet (he inherited this title from his father along with the word 'Sir') and OBE (for human endeavour and charitable services) is one of Britain's best-known explorers. Perhaps his most famous trip was the transglobe expedition undertaken between 1979 and 1982, where he journeyed around the world on its polar axis, using surface transport only, along with fellow explorer Charles Burton.

Together they covered more than 52,000 miles and became the first men to have visited both poles. Previous feats of extraordinary exploration had included a journey up the White Nile on a hovercraft, the discovery of the lost city of Ubar in Oman, an attempt to climb Everest (he reached 28,500ft) and most recently, the completion of seven marathons, in seven days, on seven continents despite having heart surgery four months earlier. Not content with just being an explorer, Fiennes has also written several books, taken part in the European elections, runs a sheep and cattle farm on Exmoor, and was once on a shortlist to replace Sean Connery in the role of James Bond.

Yet he has somehow found some time to praise the Scouts and the invaluable skills its gave him: 'The first thing you learn [as a climber] is to make sure that the knots you tie are secure... and you know how to tie them,' he said in a recent interview. 'Unfortunately, I've got a bad memory and if a few months have gone by since the last knot-tying sessions, I will get them wrong – with one life-saving exception. And that is when I was a Boy Scout way back yonder, I learnt the reef knot: left over right and right over left.' It just goes to show that knot-tying really can be useful.

THINGS ALL SCOUTS SHOULD KNOW

In everyday life, both in town and country, there are interesting 'signs' to test your scoutcraft...

from *The Scout*, No 1, Volume I, 20 June 1908

A good puncture tip

If by chance you get a puncture whilst cycling and have no glass-paper with which to clean the tube and patch, you will find a match a good substitute. Simply rub the head of the match over the rubber you wish to clean, and all the dirt will be removed. The side of an ordinary matchbox is useful for the same purpose, too, but there is a possibility that small particles from it may adhere to the rubber, and cause a minute puncture when ridden upon.

Year in the twentieth century in which Olave St Clair Baden-Powell – wife of B-P and World Chief Guide – died, on 19 June – 77

Making a scene isn't something you'd usually associate with a Scout, unless it's in a Gang Show, of course. This is the place where Scouts and Guides can put their performance skills to the test. Some love the limelight so much they go on to make a career of it.

The format of a Gang Show is generally that of a variety show. It can include comedy skits, short routine and sketches and music and dance numbers that are often of surprising sophistication.

The concept of the Gang Show was introduced by Ralph Reader in 1932, when he was just a young Rover Scout in Holborn, London. His initial motivation – apart from a relentless desire to sing, dance and be merry – was to raise funds for a swimming pool at Downe Scout Camp (now a Scout Association National Activity Centre). Spurred on by Gang Shows, Ralph went on to write a host of sketches and songs, including the signature tune 'We're Riding Along on the Crest of a Wave'. This is traditionally sung as the finale of Gang Shows around the world.

The name 'Gang Show' is said to have come about at rehearsals for the first show. When Ralph asked one member of the crew if all the cast were back from their break, and he replied: 'Aye, aye, skip, the gang's all here.'

Along with the Gang Show, Ralph is also credited with initiating a red Scout scarf that would be worn by all Gang Show members. As this concept spread throughout the world, the UK Gang Shows felt they needed to find an additional way to express their identities. Scouts can still be thespians after all. London took the lead, by embroidering the insignia 'GS London' in gold on the point of the scarf. Today, each gang wears a local Gang Show gold badge in the same place. There's just one catch – a show must have been assessed under the criteria of the Scout Show Recognition Scheme before it is granted Nationally Recognised Status, which usually lasts for three years.

Those who took part in Gang Shows and are desperate to reminisce can keep in touch through The London Gang Show Fellowship – set up by Ralph in 1972.

In 1947, Bob Monkhouse made his radio debut with the first airing of *Ralph Reader's BBC Gang Show*.

Gang Shows in the UK include: Bath and District Scout and Guide Gang Show; Blackpool Scout Gang Show; Bristol Gang Show; Harpenden Scout Gang Show; Marple Scout and Guide Gang Show; South East Berkshire Gang Show; and St Albans Scout and Guide Gang Show.

Some famous thesps and funnymen who have appeared in Gang Shows include Dicky Emery, Peter Sellers, Harry Secombe, Richard Attenborough, Max Bygraves, Spike Milligan and Tony Hancock.

78 *Increased number of beds in the Baden-Powell House Scout Activity Centre and Hostel in 1997, compared to those available since the renovation in 1961*

NIGHTS AWAY

Bashful Bill would go to any lengths to get out of singing in the Gang Show.

QUOTE UNQUOTE

I'm a professional adventurer. I have to survive off my wits. You could say that this all began age 10 to 12 as a Scout, when I first learnt to rub two sticks together, literally.
Benedict Allen, explorer and former Scout

SCOUTING TV PERSONALITIES

Sir David Attenborough • Richard Baker
Michael Barratt • David Bellamy
Sir Ralph Carr-Ellison • John Craven
Phil Gail • Russell Grant • Simon Grant
Richard Hammond • Ainsley Harriot
Natasha Kaplinsky • Ross Kemp
Richard Madley • Ray Mears
Denis Norden • Jamie Oliver
Michael Parkinson • Jeremy Paxman
Chris Tarrant • Alan Titchmarsh
Richard Whitely • Anthony Worrall Thompson

Atomic number of gold (Au) in the Periodic Table – something that all Scouts should know (although not place too much literal value to)

TO BE OR KNOT TO BE (USEFUL)

In 1977, Clinton Bailey of Pacific City, Oregon, entered the *Guinness Book of Records* for the fastest time for tying six Scout knots. He did this in 8.1 seconds. Can you beat him? You'll need to be pretty nifty with the following knots (some of their uses are included so as not to render the amount of practising you will need to do generally useless, although some may even find this jargon baffling):

Knot	Usefulness
Square knot	End lashings, tie bandages
Tautline	Adjustable loop single line (tent and tarp lines)
Bowline	Rescue loop – will not slip
Two half hitches	Attach rope to a pole or eye
Timber hitch	Begin diagonal lashing
Clove hitch	Begin square lashing

SCOUTS OF THE WORLD: FIGHTING FIRES IN FRANCE

Keeping the Scout Promise to 'help others', as part of Scouts of the World...

In the South of France, there is a Mediterranean climate, warm and dry in summer. The forest is mainly made of pines and plants, which burn very easily. A combination of drought, hot temperatures, inflammable vegetation and strong wind form an explosive mixture and something as small as a badly extinguished cigarette can easily trigger a huge forest fire. Although fighting fires is best left to the professionals, one French Scout, Alex, found that there was something he could do to help. He called young people to join the Scouts for a weekend of forest cleaning in Provence. By taking away dead trees and cutting brushwood, they could at least make the forest more accessible if the firefighters needed to get in. More than 10,000 people responded to help. Alex then decided that visitors to such areas needed to be educated to prevent fires happening in the first place. He invited Scouts from other countries to come and help spread the word, working in the most threatened areas. They organised 'fire watch' and set up patrols to look out for irresponsibly lit campfires and smoking. Since then, similar projects have been set up in countries such as Sicily and Spain, allowing Scouts there to help protect their environment, and gain new skills.

 Year in the twentieth century in which Gerry Rafferty recorded the song 'I was a Boy Scout', part of his Snakes and Ladders *album*

ONE RAINY NIGHT AT SCOUT CAMP

It can sometimes be a bit boring at camp if it's wet. But worry not – John Sweet, writing in *The Scout*, 29 June 1950 suggests devising ways to make the following inventions come true – and thus making a fortune for you and your fellow Scouts (obviously the inventor of the world wide web was at a different camp that night).

1. A telephone instrument which can be spoken into without the speaker's voice being heard in the same room.
2. A device to prevent people being run over.
3. A device to stir the contents of cooking pots automatically, e.g. by hot-air motion.
4. An invention to indicate to the bus conductor how many seats are free on the top deck.
5. A device to change typewriter ribbons without soiling one's fingers.
6. A gadget to prevent people slipping in the bath-tub.
7. 'Breathing' rails which do away with the jolts by filling the small gap between the rail and the next. (Note: Don't forget temperature fluctuations!)
8. Apparatus to enable everybody to do his own paper-hanging.
9. Crockery which is so cheap it can be thrown away after use to obviate washing up.
10. Camera which adjusts itself automatically to different lighting conditions.

BANDS WHO HAVE GING GANGED

The song 'Ging Gang Goolie', has been recorded by a number of artists. They include:

The Tremeloes
The Megatons
Karl Denver
The Rutles

Other well-known musicians may have sung the song at some time, although no one else was forthcoming with this information at the time. Trying to imagine former Scouts such as Syd Barrett and Jarvis Cocker putting their heart into an 'Oompah' is perhaps one thought left well alone (they probably sang 'Ging gang goolie goolie goolie on a pushbike...' anyway). Paul McCartney did however come close with his hit 'We All Stand Together', written for the film *Rupert and the Frog Song* (1985).

KEY SCOUTING DATES: 1950s

1950

November Scouts are forbidden to hitchhike except for in emergencies.

December *The London Gang Show* is revived for the first time since the war.

1952

April Queen Elizabeth II (she will be crowned in 1953) reviews the national parade of Queen's Scouts at Windsor Castle and takes the salute for the first time.

1954

March Debate in the House of Lords on the Scout Movement and Communism.

1956

February International Scout Club is formed.

June A new musical play by Ralph Reader, *Voyage of the Venturer*, is performed by the London Scouts and Guides in the Royal Albert Hall.

1959

February The Boy Scout Association announces that it will join the Duke of Edinburgh's Award Scheme.

SCOUT'S HORROR: AN UNHAPPY ENDING

No *Scouting Companion* would be complete without a few Scouting nightmares, sad yarns, odd tales and wicked deeds, just to balance the books. The tellers of these anecdotes wish to remain anonymous just in case the Scouts come and make them do some good turns.

'There was the time I ran out of water on a roasting hot day on the dreaded 15-mile hike, my Scout Leader told us you could drink water from freshwater streams – so long as the pebbles the water ran over were free of algae all should be well. We crossed a stream, I filled my canteen and drank the lot in about 20 seconds. Of course, then my mate finds a dead fish floating just upstream of me. Cut to five hours later and I'm sitting upright in the centre pole of the tent, groaning, with a wide circle of Scouts as far away from me as possible and bodily detritus everywhere. When my parents arrived for the open day they were greeted at the gate with, "Hello, Mr and Mrs [Anon], your son has dysentery".'

A Photographer

 Last two digits in the number for the Kandersteg Chalet, an International Scout Centre in the Swiss Alps, since 1921; the number is +41 33 675 82 82

THE CAMP COOK: BROILED FISH

From *Backwoods Cooking – Practical Methods and Recipes*, a reprint of a popular collection that first appeared in *Scouting* magazine.

You will need:

- A supply of greensticks
- One fish per person

Method:

1. Prepare the fish (gut, remove bones, slit down centre).
2. Strip the bark off the greensticks you are to use and seal them by placing them briefly over hot coals.
3. Find a large Y-shaped greenstick (ash, hazel or willow are suitable, not holly or yew) and weave it into a tennis racket shape.
4. Open out the gutted fish and place it upon three sticks laid lengthways on the 'racket'.
5. Lay a further three or four sticks across the top of the fish, at right angles to the other sticks, tucking the ends underneath the sides of the 'racket' as shown, to keep the fish in place.
6. Prop the broiler a short distance above the glowing coals and cook for about 20 minutes, turning occasionally.

QUOTE UNQUOTE

A good picture is equivalent to a good deed.
Vincent Van Gogh, Dutch artist

A BRIEF NOTE ABOUT KNOTS

If you are training a tenderfoot, just learning knots will not do, as an article in *The Scout*, 13 October 1949, explains...

When you get around to knotting, try to show the uses. Just tying a knot and telling the chap its uses often confuses him, but if you actually do a few things, such as lowering weights from heights, mooring a boat or tying a bandage, he stands a better chance of remembering the right answers.

And do not miss whipping! I have seen several cases where the recruit laboriously learns the knots, then at the last moment he is told, 'Whipping is easy, you do it like this', and he is rushed off to pass the test without a chance to practice it–hence the large amount of rope which quickly ends its days as 'cows' tails' in many troop rooms (not yours, of course!).

THE ORIGINAL GRAND HOWL

When the Wolf Cubs began in 1916, Baden-Powell designed a Grand Howl that Cubs and Leaders could use to greet each other with at the start of each meeting. The Howl would also be used at ceremonies and as to honour a visitor to the Pack – the highest accolade that could be given. From the Howl came the 'dyb-dyb-dyb' that defines the Scouts for many today.

Start squatted hands between feet
All Cubs: Ah-kay-la! – We'll do our **best**.
Cubs spring to their feet, with two fingers of each hand pointing upwards at each side of head, to look like two wolf's ears.
Leading Cub: Dyb-dyb-dyb-dyb (meaning 'do your best')
After the fourth 'dyb', each Cub drops his left hand smartly to his side, spreads his fingers into the salute with his right hand, and squeals
All Cubs: We'll
and barks
All Cubs: Dob-dob-dob-dob (meaning 'do our best')
On the fourth 'dob', each Cub drops his right hand smartly to his side, and is now standing at the alert waiting for further orders.

HUNGRY LIKE THE WOLF CUB

Backwoods cooking for beginners – not to be attempted by adults unless under the expert supervision of a qualified Cub:

Instant hot dogs
Lay sliced onion on a small, double-thickness, layer of foil, add a sausage and wrap up the foil, sealing the ends tightly (and making sure there is still a fair amount of air left inside the package). Place in hot embers for about seven minutes, onion side down (so that the sausage does not stick to the foil) and, when cooked, pop the meat and onions into a bread roll for a quick and easy hot dog.

Simple kebab
Remove the bark from a thin greenstick and spear slices of bacon, mushrooms, sausage, carrot and peppers on to it. Support the skewer over glowing embers, turning occasionally, and remove when the meat is crisp and golden brown.

Pineapple pud
Slice the top off a fresh pineapple and, using a sharp knife and a spoon, carefully remove the centre. Fill this with a mixture of sultanas, pineapple, sliced apple and grated chocolate, replace the top of the pineapple, securing it in place with two small sticks, and bury in hot embers for about 30 minutes.

 Percentage of 1,004 13-18-year-olds stating that looking after the environment was important, found in research by The Scout Association in 2007

THINGS ALL SCOUTS SHOULD KNOW

In everyday life, both in town and country, there are interesting 'signs' to test your scoutcraft...
from *The Scout*, No 1, Volume I, 16 May 1908

New use for a thimble

Here is a hint that should be known in every house. When putting a rod through the hem of a curtain, the stick is liable to tear it. Anyway, it does not generally slip through easily. But just put a thimble on one end of the stick, and you will find it will glide through without causing any inconvenience.

STRANGE MEETING PLACES

In the early years of Scouting, a Meeting Place often had to be improvised. Here are just some of the places where the first meetings were held:

Disused laundry ....1st Pinner Green Troop, 1929

Local hospital society's hut ....22nd Stretford (Manchester) Troop, 1945

Old corrugated iron hut.............75th North London (Lord Cooper's Own) Troop, 1922

Disused railway station..............Southwold Scout Troop, 1935

Army hut ....35th Sheffield (St Oswald's) Troop

Under a lamp-post ....24th East Belfast Troop (come rain, hail or snow)

MOMENTOUS MORSE

Winston Churchill is well known for using the 'V' sign to represent victory and peace and urge the side on. What he did with his hands, the BBC wanted to do with the radio, but how? Apparently Douglas Ritchie of the BBC European Service suggested an audible 'V' using that Scout favourite, the Morse code rhythm. The Morse code for the letter 'V' is '... –', three dots and a dash. This is also rhythm for the opening bars of Beethoven's Fifth Symphony, and was used as the call-sign by the BBC in its foreign language programmes to occupied Europe throughout the war. The ironic use of a German composition, to add further insult, was not lost.

Cost in pounds for each British Scout who took park in the 11th World Scout Jamboree, held in Marathon, Greece, in 1963

Books of instruction and general interest, and their reviews in the press suggested in Robert Baden-Powell's *Boy Scouts Beyond the Seas: My World Tour*, 1913.

Yarns for Boy Scouts
by Robert Baden-Powell
'There is no gift book that could be put into the hands of a schoolboy more valuable than this fascinating volume, and if you asked the boy's opinion he would probably add, "no book that he liked better".' – *Spectator*

Scouting Games
by Robert Baden-Powell
'No one who, as a schoolboy, has read a word of Fenimore Cooper or Ballantyne, nobody who feels the fascination of a good detective story, or who understands a little of the pleasures of woodcraft could fail to be attracted by these games or, for that matter, by the playing of the games themselves.' – *Spectator*

Things All Scouts Should Know
A series of 313 illustrated paragraphs about the Army and Navy, ships and boats, flag and other signals, railways, cycling, camping, hobbies, etc.

Woodcraft
By Owen Jones and Marcus Woodward
'Packed from end to end with observations and instructions which turn the countryside and its small inhabitants from a series of perplexing puzzles into a vast book which every intelligent person can read for himself.' – *The Globe*

Going About the Country with Your Eyes Open
by Owen Jones and Marcus Woodward
'A delightfully varied volume dealing with topics full of interest and also of instruction to those who knock about the country.' – *Morning Post*

My Tightest Corner
'A welcome and even valuable addition to the Scout library, for the chief actors in the scenes and incidents recounted themselves fight their battles all over again. Adventures ashore and afloat, perils from men and beasts, suffering and privation, and the facing of grievous odds are the key-notes to the various stories, which show the young reader again and again how cool self-reliance more often than not brings a man out of the tightest of corners.' – *Field*

The Scout as Handy Man
This volume contains instructions for those wishing to obtain the Handy Man badge. It is very fully illustrated with diagrams and gives reliable information on the following subjects among others: painting and whitewashing, repairing gas fittings, ball cocks, tap-washers, sashlines, window and door fastenings, Venetian blinds, etc. Many besides Scouts will find an exceedingly useful volume of information.

 Year in the twentieth century in which the Beaver Scouts were given their own Promise, and became an official part of The UK Scout Association

NIGHTS AWAY

Jake's first attempt to get his Explorer's Badge saw him take the short cut to the North Pole. He came down a hero.

LONG LIVE THE *BADEN-POWELL*!

'It might almost have been the first Sea Scouts' boat, but it pre-dated the formation of the Scout Movement by almost 10 years...'

So began the introduction to a feature about the fishing boat, *Baden-Powell*, in a millennium edition of *Scouting* magazine. Now over 100 years old, the *Baden-Powell* was named after the hero of Mafeking and has kept its name throughout its life. Built in King's Lynn in Norfolk in 1901 by the Worfolk Brothers, it is a typical cockle fishing yawl, 33ft long with a beam of 11ft. A sturdy vessel, it fished the waters of The Wash for over 95 years. Sadly, the *Baden-Powell* nearly returned to timber some five years ago when funds could not be found to maintain her. But now with the help of the Trues Yard Fishing Heritage Museum it is hoped that she can be restored and ride the waves again – this time as a leisure boat, taking visitors out on this beautiful strip of coast.

Year in the twentieth century when 250 Scouts from Greater London North East enter the record books by cooking a world-record 14.5km sausage

NOTES FROM THE FOUNDER

B-P on mountaineering...

I have pettifogged freely up and down the minor heights of the Himalayas and the Andes and the Rockies, but though I have gazed in awed admiration on their mighty snows, I have never trespassed on their sublime heights.

There is to me something sacred about their calm isolation far far above the world where it would be presumption for puny man to make his footsteps.

Robert Baden-Powell,
***Lessons from the Varsity of Life*, 1933**

SCOUTS UNITED

Look hard at the three words below.
Can you find the missing link?

- Alpine butterfly
- Dogshank
- Cat's Paw

Answer on page 153.

BOB'S YOUR UNCLE

'In order to get money you must expect to work.' So said Baden-Powell in *Scouting for Boys* and more than 40 years later 'Bob-A-Job' week was born.

An article in *The Scouter* presented the idea to its Patrol Leaders in 1949 as a 'grand chance to earn money while the public eye is focused upon us'. As well as being a prime publicity stunt, it also gave Scouts the opportunity to exercise the third Scout Law – a way to do something extra for other people, without any personal reward.

Scouts were required to wear uniform while on the job, or at least a Scout buttonhole badge. They were also given job cards with space for up to 12 jobs – quite a target to set for one week. Keen jobbers could even have a second card if they wished.

For each job Scouts would earn a 'bob' (slang for a shilling) – the equivalent of about 5p – and this would go towards Scout funds. However Scout headquarters knew the famous 'Bob-A-Job' slogan would lose its worth in 1971 thanks to decimalisation and therefore changed the name to Scout Job Week in 1970.

 Number of Devon Cubs, Scouts and parents taken on an adventure camping holiday in Canada, courtesy of Scout Leader Lotto winner Paul Bristow

SCOUTING FOR ASBOS

It may come about in life that one feels the need to seek advice in order to combat anti-social leanings and habits such as a quick temper. One such Scout wrote to *The Scout* on 2 March 1950 expressing that whenever he felt annoyed or angry he had the 'urge to knock someone's block off'. He promptly received the following reply from the editor, which might prove useful to equally frustrated youths of today.

'B-P once told the story of a man who had a remedy for a rising temper. This man said that on a surge of anger coming on you should take off your coat and begin some exercises – like those given in *Scouting for Boys* for making yourself strong – stretch and bend, twist your body round with arms extended, bend forward and touch your toes, keeping the knees stiff.

'If you have not by that time got rid of your rage, take your pillow, kick it around the room, and you are bound to feel all right, "good and kind" in no time.

'Commenting on that, B-P said that Scouts didn't need to do all that to beat a bad temper. They know what a smile and whistle will do. It cannot fail, he said, if you have a strong enough will to make yourself whistle a tune when you are very angry; it is bound to set you right in less that a minute – especially if you don't forget to grin, too!'

SCOUT'S HORROR: BACK TO THE BEACH

No *Scout's Companion* would be complete without a few Scouting nightmares, sad yarns, odd tales and wicked deeds, just to balance the books. The tellers of these anecdotes wish to remain anonymous, just in case the Scouts come and make them do some good turns.

'Our Cubs had two annual camps: summer and winter. Winter camp was held in a hut near a chalk pit in Fairlight, East Sussex. The place was surrounded by burnt-out cars and biker gangs. I liked it. We learnt how to abseil and walked along the cliffs and the beach. In the Scout van (a Ford transit with the Scout logo), the Scouts – who always seemed to be about – were really into Adam and the Ants and The Specials so we used to sing "Ant People" and "Much Too Much" a lot. One time, my snorkel parker got too close to a radiator and melted on the arm and my mum was really angry. A couple of years ago some friends asked me if I knew any good, secluded beaches in Sussex. I suggested Fairlight. They went only to find it is now a nudist colony. They assumed I was playing a joke on them.'

A Curator

Year in the twentieth century in which former Scout Steven Spielberg launched the Merit Badge for Cinematography in the US

NAUGHTY KNEES

A classified ad from an issue of *The Scouter*, 1950:

Discipline – Dress – Delinquincy!
These are subjects in which you are vitally interested as a Scouter!
Are you for or against spanking? Do you agree with shorts up to the age of 15? Can delinquents be reclaimed by Scouting?
These are subjects frankly discussed in

CRIME IN SHORTS

Post free 1/9 from
The Publishers, 335 City Road,
London, EC1

[Reviewed in *The Scouter* and *Daily Mirror*]

LOST AND FOUND

When 10,000 Scouts from 68 countries departed Hylands Park at the end of EuroJam in summer 2005, two whole transit van-loads of 'lost and found' were recovered by the Jamboree Team. Lost property included £400 in cash, sunglasses, sleeping bags, carry mats and perhaps most oddly – several left and right boots. Observing the 1st Scout Law 'A Scout is to be trusted', it was attempted to reunite any leftover items with their rightful owners. Digital cameras were particularly easy to trace back as staff could identify Troops by pictures of telltale uniforms. The nationalities of some wallet owners could also be identified by the currency contained within.

But this was not the first experience of 'lost and found' for the Scouts. The US Scouting site www.pintreeweb.com tells of lost property at the 4th World Jamboree in Gödöllö, Hungary, in 1933, with 'lost and found' signs in many languages on a booth in Elizabeth Street. Some of the items left there were cameras, hats, toothbrushes and axes. At the first World Scout Jamboree in London, England, in 1920, it was the same story with 'cameras, purses with money in them, toothbrushes (nearly 100 of them, and mostly still unclaimed, worse luck), and even the kilt of a Scottish Officer.' The editor of the website writes that, after the event, the Chief Scout wrote in the office register: 'This is the finest example of the keeping of the first Scout law I have ever seen.'

With 40,000 Scouts expected to attend the 21st World Scout Jamboree in 2007, let's hope they go prepared and remember to put their names on everything.

 Year in the twentieth century in which the decision was made to allow girls into the UK Beaver Scout, Cub Scout and Scout sections

PATROL NAMES AND THEIR PECULIARITIES: THE PEEWIT

As referred to in an enlightening series by JR Stanley (author of *Five Boys and a Master*) in *The Scouter*, January 1930:

- The peewit is a bird of temperate climes, often being found in North Asia.
- The peewit is famed for its unorthodox plumage of green, white and brown, with a beautiful curved crest to give the finishing touch.
- The peewit is about the same size as a pigeon.
- From its habit of curling the wings when flying, the peewit is often referred to as the lapwing.
- The peewit is fond of wide open spaces of ploughland and meadow where he breeds; in winter peewits haunt the seashore in flocks.
- Four eggs, pear-shaped and drab, with blotches of black are laid in a slight hollow in the ground.
- The peewit bird never takes cover and is constantly searching for insects and birds.
- The pretty, fluffy young of the peewit are able to run and feed immediately after hatching.
- The peewit will follow any intruders – even man or dog – if it feels there is a danger near its nest.
- The peewit makes a peculiar swish-swish-swish sound with its flapping wings as the wind passes through its pinion feathers.

TEAM DESERT SCOUTS

Few people would dare cross England in a car worth less than £100. But three brave Scout Leaders are marking Scouting's Centenary by taking their banger to greater extremes – by driving it 4,000 miles from the south coast of England, across France, Andorra, Spain, Morocco and the Sahara Desert, as part of the Plymouth to Banjul Challenge. Teams could only spend £15 on doing up their vehicle, not much considering the obstacles they might face on the way. But Team Desert Scout would not be put off by these restrictions: their website reported a successful arrival in Banjul on 10 January 2007 – even after one passport went missing and someone mistakenly filled up their car with diesel. They raised £2,100 in total. The first £1,000 came from the auction of their car in Gambia and this went to Gambian charities. A second amount of £1,100 was donated to the Winchester Children's Hospice.

Year in the twentieth century in which the film The Last Boy Scout *was premiered; title aside, the film has nothing to do with the Scouts at all*

AN A-Z OF ACTIVITY BADGES: I-M

This most up-to-date list of Scout Activity Badges proves there's more than one reason to join the Scouts. The list is provided in bite-sized pieces throughout the book so as not to get badge addicts too over-excited.

- Information Technology (staged)
- Interpreter
- Librarian
- Lifesaver
- Martial Arts
- Master at Arms
- Mechanic
- Meteorologist
- Model Maker
- Musician (staged)
- My Faith

QUOTE UNQUOTE

A War Service badge was instituted in 1914; it was awarded to Scouts doing at least 28 days of service of three hours a day; some 70,000 of these badges were earned by 1918. There was also a special 100 Days badge.

EE Reynolds, *Boy Scout Jubilee*, 1957

WHOSE BADGE IS IT ANYWAY?

You might have a full arm of new badges. Or you may be taking a trip down memory lane. But can you guess what this Cub Scout Proficiency Badge is for?

a) Artist
b) Painter and decorator
c) Milliner

Answer on page 153.

 Percentage of young people in a 2001 survey by British Meat – sponsors of the Cub Scout and Scout Cook Badges – who said they liked to cook

THE SCOUT MOTTO

The Scout Motto is: *Be prepared*
If you forget this motto then you are not observing it correctly.

A ROYAL STAMP OF APPROVAL

September 2006 saw the release of six postage stamps to commemorate the 150th anniversary of the Victoria Cross. On one of the stamps was the face of one boy seamen first-class, Jack Cornwell. He was only 16 when he died on 31 May 1916, when his boat the *HMS Chester* was set upon by four enemy cruisers at the Battle of Jutland. He received a posthumous Victoria Cross for remaining at his gun turret even though he was fatally wounded. In a letter to his mother after the battle his captain wrote of him: 'He remained stead at his most exposed post… he felt that he might be needed and indeed he might have been; so he stayed there, standing and waiting, under heavy fire, with just his own brave heart and God's help to support him.'

A keen member of the Scouts and all they stood for, Jack was also acknowledged by the Movement, with the establishment of the Cornwell Scout Badge in his memory. Admiral Lord Beresford wrote in the *Boy's Own Paper* at the time: 'Cornwell has set an example of devotion to duty which will be an inspiration to British boys for all time.'

The Cornwell Scout Badge was introduced in the *Headquarters Gazette* along with the criteria for gaining the award. This included 'passing a test of physical courage' such as boxing or high-diving, although the Scout in question must already be a first-class Scout, have passed the Missioner's Badge (as Jack had before) and hold two other Proficiency Badges from a select list.

Several readers wrote back, saying that the badge should in fact be awarded for an act of 'real valour'. But Baden-Powell was determined that bravery and courage could be aimed for, and that these qualities could be practised by treating the award as a Proficiency Badge. He made the first presentation of the Cornwell Scout Badge to a Patrol Leader, in front of an audience of 4,000 in Middlesborough, 1 November 1916.

Today the badge is awarded in respect of pre-eminently high character, devotion to duty, together with great courage and endurance. The bronze badge or cloth emblem can be won by all youth members of The Scout Association, from Beavers to Scout Network Members.

Royal Mail has chosen the Centenary of Scouting as its subject for a set of six stamps to be launched in July 2007. Scouting beat competition from almost 2,000 other entries.

Size in hectares of Scout Valley, a nature park near the city of Orillia in Simcoe County, Oregon; it takes its name from the many Scout camps there

NOTES FROM THE FOUNDER

B-P on the Scout law...

So the Scout law was not formed as a list of **don'ts**. Prohibition generally invites evasion since it challenges the spirit inherent in every red-blooded boy (or man).

The boy is not governed by **don't**, but is led on by **do**. The Scout law, therefore, was devised as a guide to his actions rather than a repressive of his faults. It merely states what is good form and expected as a Scout.

1. A Scout's honour is to be trusted.
2. A Scout is loyal.
3. A Scout's duty is to be useful.
4. A Scout is a friend to all.
5. A Scout is courteous.
6. A Scout is a friend to animals.
7. A Scout obeys orders.
8. A Scout smiles and whistles under all difficulties.
9. A Scout is thrifty.
10. A Scout is clean in thought, word and deed.

Lord Baden-Powell of Gilwell,
***Lessons from the Varsity of Life*, 1933**

PIRATE PATROL

If you've ever been tempted to download some freebies from Napster or Limewire watch out that you don't do it with an LA Boy Scout in the room – they might report you in the name of a new badge launched in 2006. Launched by the Motion Picture Association of America and the Los Angeles Boy Scouts, the anti-piracy badge – officially named the Respect Copyrights patch – has been designed to help raise awareness about respecting copyrights and change attitudes towards intellectual property theft. For those young Scouts who don't include the phrase 'intellectual property' in their everyday slang, it refers to the concept that 'ideas' are valuable, they can be owned and protected from other people stealing them by copyrighting, trademarking or patenting. The badge aims to teach kids how to identify counterfeit CDs and DVDs, the consequences of film and music piracy and that protecting them is important to their local economy. If the scheme is a success it will be launched to other Scouts between six and 21 years old throughout California and the rest of America, although a closer look at the 'acquired' playlists of some Scouts' iPods might open a whole new can of worms.

 Year in the twentieth century in which the 1st Russian International Jamboree took place in St Petersburg

THE CAMP COOK: MAGIC PIE

From *Backwoods Cooking – Practical Methods and Recipes*, a reprint of a popular collection that first appeared in *Scouting* magazine.

You will need:

- 4 eggs
- 1/2 cup plain flour
- 2 cups milk
- 2 tsp vanilla essence
- 1/2 cup margarine
- 1/2 cup sugar
- 1 cup desiccated coconut

Method:

1. Beat the eggs and gradually stir in the flour.
2. Mix in the rest of the ingredients and pour the mixture into a dish made from a double-thickness layer of foil.
3. Bake in a camp oven for approximately one hour or until the centre of the pie is firm.
4. The magic pie is so called because, as it is cooked, the flour settles to form a crusty base, the coconut rises to make the topping leaving an egg custard mix in the centre.

Note:

The recipe here uses 'cups' as the standard means of measurement. This is perhaps an easier system to use at camp, as long as the same cup or mug is used throughout the recipe to ensure the correct ratio of ingredients.

ON YER BIKE

Jean-Michel 'Jean-Mi' Chalon was one Scout who wanted to show young people that being a Scout is to follow your dreams to the end, and to achieve them whatever unforeseen obstacles may appear on the road along the way. To prove his point he decided to cycle around the Med (OK, so it was also a bet). On his tour he traversed a range of terrains in Spain, Morocco, Algeria, Tunisia, Egypt, Israel, Cyprus, Greece, Albania, Montenegro, Croatia, Bosnia, Slovenia, Italy and Switzerland. As well as promoting the Scouts along the way, Jean-Mi also had another mission in mind. He collected as many tree samples as he could under the premise that: 'Scouts are the gardeners of the world, and the young growths of today are the forests of tomorrow.' It is not certain where he is at with his forest but if it does come together, it is sure to be an exotic collection of species.

Year in the twentieth century in which former Scout Jarvis Cocker released the single 'Common People'

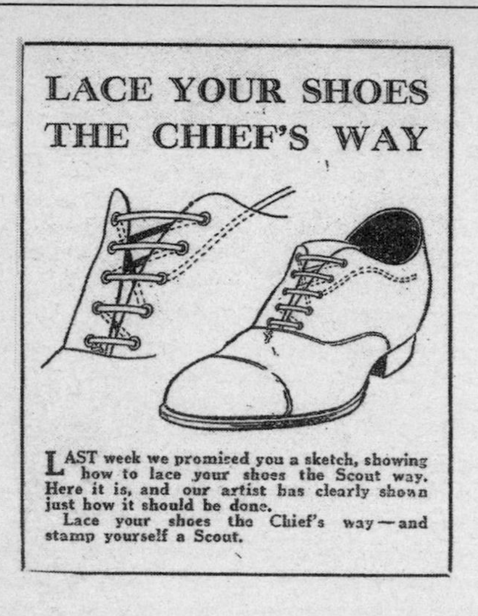

LACE YOUR SHOES THE CHIEF'S WAY

LAST week we promised you a sketch, showing how to lace your shoes the Scout way. Here it is, and our artist has clearly shown just how it should be done.

Lace your shoes the Chief's way—and stamp yourself a Scout.

THINGS ALL SCOUTS SHOULD KNOW

In everyday life, both in town and country, there are interesting 'signs' to test your scoutcraft...
from *The Scout*, No 1, Volume I, 23 May 1908

Why hollow trees live

In forests and private parks, one may often witness the remarkable sight of a very old tree, with a trunk consisting of nothing but a hollow shell, and yet bearing branches that are covered with foliage.

It would seem impossible that the dry bark, in some cases only held together by an iron band, could go on producing leaves year after year in the manner in which it does.

The explanation, however, is quite a simple one. In very young trees, the sap-carrying portion is in the centre. It is a series of bundles of minute cellular tubes. As the tree gets older these tubes form a ring which gets bigger and bigger as the circumference of the tree increases. In course of time the centre withdraws and decays, since it is no longer needed to supply the branches with nourishment.

 Year in the twentieth century in which the first official Scout website was launched – www.scoutbase.org.uk. It is now www.scouts.org.uk

READY, STEADY, SCOUT: PART III

Contrary to popular belief, the Scouts was not established as an 'organisation' but rather more organic in its spread, picking up legions of fans along the way. The first Scout census of 1910 would count a phenomenal 100,000 members. Here, Baden-Powell tells his own account of how it all began, in 'How I started Scouting', *The Scout*, No 1, Volume I, 18 April 1908...

We not only sailed our boat round most of the coast of England, but we also made boat expeditions inland in a small folding canvas boat, which was great fun. We explored the Thames pretty nearly up to its source in the Chiltern Hills, and we got on to the Avon, which rises the other side of the same hills, and went down it through Bath and Bristol to the Severn; then we crossed the Severn and went up the Wye into Wales. We carried our tent and cooking pots with us and slept out in camps every night, and had a real good time.

Handy men all

Of course, to do this we all had to be 'handy men' – to understand all about rowing and managing the boat, how to swim, how to tie knots, how to light fires and cook food, how to build shelters and to drain a wet camp, and so on. We used to get leave from the owner of the land where we stopped to take a rabbit or catch some fish for food. To get a rabbit we either set a snare or, what was better fun, we stalked him with a little saloon pistol.

One evening I was doing this at a place where, I am sorry to say, we had not got leave. There was no house to be seen, and we were late and short of food.

I was creeping up behind a bush to get within shot of a fine rabbit who was squatting in the grass, when I thought I heard a crackling of leaves and sticks the other side of the bush. A horrible idea struck me that a keeper was there stalking me, so I quickly slid back and crept away again as quietly as I could. When I had gone some little distance I squirmed round, still lying flat on the ground, to see if I was being followed, and then I saw another fellow creeping away from the bush in the opposite direction.

He, too, was a poacher, who had likewise heard me and thought I was a keeper, and we were both wriggling away from each other! So I had another look at the rabbit, and he, cunning beggar, was sitting there, and I could almost swear he was giggling; at any rate, the next moment he popped into his hole, and we got no rabbit for supper that night.

Year in the nineteenth century in which Scouts took on the task of redistributing the gifts and flowers left by Princess Diana's mourners

CELEBRITY SCOUTS: RUSSELL GRANT

What this famous Scout did next...

Whether you subscribe to the wonders of astrology or not (Baden-Powell tellingly referred to the practice as 'ass-trology' in his book *Paddle Your Own Canoe or Tips for Boys – From the Jungle and Elsewhere*, 1939) you can't help but salute Russell Grant's meteoric rise to success. The former teenage star of stage and screen – appearances include the BBC's *Canterbury Tales* and *Please Sir!* – was first taken under the wing of Rita Szymanski, the then-treasurer of the Astrological Lodge of Great Britain. While there, he rubbed shoulders with other stellar psychics, including Doris Stokes. In 1978, his veritable rise to stardom was confirmed with a reading for the Queen Mother in public. It seems the planets have been stacked in his favour ever since. He was awarded the title of Royal Astrologer for the first time in 300 years. Global success was soon to follow with slots on primetime TV on both sides of the Atlantic, and a syndicated column to more than 450 newspapers worldwide. Best-selling books were next, followed by a website that is said to attract up to 10 million visitors every month. For this Russell deserves both a badge for Astrology and one for Public Relations. In true Scouting fashion, Russell also has his finger in a few other pies: not least as author of *The Real Counties of Britain* (notable in that it commissioned Ordnance Survey to produce maps of the traditional counties of England, Scotland and Wales) and as patron of County Conservation. As owner of the manorial title Lord of the Manor of Ashford of Middlesex he also maintains a strong aptitude for another Scouting legacy, collecting – namely, other places called Middlesex around the world.

WHISTLE WHILE YOU WORK

Just a few ways in which Scouts could 'Bob-A-Job' in 1950, as described in an issue of *The Scouter*:

Carting manure and turf
Cutting grass on graves
Cycle-cleaning
Digging
Firewood-chopping
Messages
Mowing lawns
Pea-stick collecting
Polishing woodwork
Road mending
Shoe and boot-cleaning
Shopping
Subscriptions
Washing dishes
Weeding
Whitewashing

 Year in the twentieth century that the first JOTT – Jamboree on the Trail – took place; Scouts in different countries walked together worldwide

SCOUT'S HORROR: THE MYSTERY BAG

No *Scout's Companion* would be complete without a few Scouting nightmares, sad yarns, odd tales and wicked deeds, just to balance the books. The tellers of these anecdotes wish to remain anonymous just in case the Scouts come and make them do some good turns.

'When we joined we were given a plastic bag with Cub Rules, a poster and other things that we never read. Each meeting we had to bring this bag, together with a handkerchief, a piece of string and a 10-pence piece. These were so that we would be able to follow the motto and "be prepared".

'My handkerchief was a paper one. It was supposed to be for making a bandage, but I guess my mum thought it was in case we needed to sneeze. The 10-pence piece was for making a phone call. Not sure about the string.' **A Curator**

QUOTE UNQUOTE

On my honour, I'll do my best.
George W Bush, US president and former Scout, speaking at 2005 National Boy Scout Jamboree in the US

IS SCOUTING GOOD FOR YOU?

It's a controversial one, it's true. Steadfast Scout fans would argue that it was their only chance to experience the great outdoors, try new activities and meet like-minded people. They usually have a fondness for knots, love saluting, and you can still find some of them Scouting well into later life. Others may say their experiences of camping out had ruined the outdoors for them for life. You will never catch them in shorts, they have an innate fear of badges and will never, ever, ever be seen in green. But one report unveiled in *The Sunday Times*, 22 October 2006, and conducted by the Institute for Public Policy Research does attempt to qualify Scouting's 'goodness'. It found that 'former Scouts and Guides were three per cent less likely to be depressed and five per cent less likely to be single, separated or divorced by the age of 30'. They were 'also more likely to own a home, achieve good qualifications and be earning a decent income, even after correcting for their class background'. The Institute believed the results of the report were so strong that the government should incorporate Scouting into the nation's National Curriculum.

Having read the report, the author of this book is now seriously considering donning a woggle and rejoining the Scout Movement in a bid to make it onto the property ladder.

KEY SCOUTING DATES: 1960s

	1961
November	Long trousers are introduced as alternative wear for senior Scout Troops and Rover Scout crews.
	1962
August	First exchange visit of Scouts with the USA.
	1966
September	*The Scout* magazine ceases publication.
	1967
May	The Boy Scouts Association is renamed The Scout Association.
October	New uniform is introduced. Senior Scouts and Rover Scouts are phased out in favour of Venture Scouts.
	1968
January	Prince Andrew joins the 1st Marylebone Cub Scout Pack; for the duration of his membership, the Pack meet at Buckingham Palace.

QUOTE UNQUOTE

Badges, we don't need no stinking badges!
Mexican bandit in the film *Blazing Saddles* (1974), a spoof of the original line from *The Treasure of the Sierra Madre* (1948)

SCOUTS OF THE WORLD: AWAY WITH VIOLENCE IN SALVADOR

Keeping the Scout Promise to 'help others'...

Many young people in El Salvador are trapped in a culture of violence, due in part to the civil war that raged for many years and internal migration from rural land to the cities. Street fights, rape and murder subsequently increased. Some local Scouts came up with the idea that the Scout Movement and gangs shared something in common: a desire to integrate with other youths. They bravely invited students aged between 15-20 years, and from rival gangs, to attend a holiday camp, swapping street fighting for fun, adventure and a chance to get out of the city. The camp experience was a huge success. It was then followed up in school and a programme rolled out across the country. There has since been an 80% reduction in student-related violence there.

 As at 2007, age in years of Scouting since B-P began the Movement in 1907

SCOUTING SKILLS: LIGHTING A FIRE

Skills to help you survive the wild, by Sir Ranulph Fiennes from *100 Years of Scouting* DVD (Endemol, 2007)

1. Make sure your matches are dry – keep them in a plastic bag inside a plastic box.
2. Build your fire away from the wind.
3. Ensure everything you want to do with the fire can be done in the place that you do it – check there is wood nearby and that water is available if you need to cook with it.
4. Don't be so keen on getting heat that you can be dangerous.

PATROL NAMES AND THEIR PECULIARITIES: THE WOOD-PIGEON

As referred to in an enlightening series by JR Stanley (author of *Five Boys and a Master*) in *The Scouter*, January 1930:

- Tame pigeons are very popular with boys.
- We have a great many more tame pigeons in the UK than wild ones.
- All pigeons are descended from the blue rock-pigeons.
- A great variety of pigeons have been formed through breeding, as the pouter, the ruff and the famous carrier pigeon.
- Pigeons are very fond of their homes and will travel miles to get back home in the quickest time possible.
- Pigeons will go hungry and thirsty to get home, and often die in their efforts to do so.
- The ring-dove, or wood-pigeon, is a shy bird in a wild state, where he does a great deal of damage to farmers' crops.
- The wood-pigeon is slightly larger than the tame pigeon.
- The wood-pigeon is a very handsome slate grey bird with a mixture of blues on the head and throat and a curious patch of white on each side of the neck and on the wings.
- The chest of the wood-pigeon is pink, as are the feet, which have three toes forward and one behind.
- Unlike most birds, young wood-pigeons do not open their beaks to receive food but insert it into the beak of the parent and take in the meal partly-digested.
- Dwellers in the country say the wood-pigeon's cooing resembles the phrase, 'Take two coooos, Paddy'.
- The official call of the wood-pigeon is 'Book–hooroo'.

THE GALLANT 30

The Scout Movement was begun with the very first experimental Scout camp organised by Baden-Powell on Brownsea Island. He organised a second camp the following year at Humshaugh, Northumberland. This time the event was advertised in *The Scout* magazine and boys were invited to nominate themselves or friends in a competition. These nominations were then subject to a voting system where the most popular entries were invited to attend. Here are the names and address of the 30 lucky winners, as published in *The Scout*, 29 August 1908...

1. **Ambler, W**, 15 Peter's Court, Mulgrave Street, Bradford.
2. **Bartlett, JS**, 11 Crosspool Street, Sheffield.
3. **Black, SS**, 46 Burngrave Road, Sheffield.
4. **Blackmorem G**, Rurtherglen, Rockingham Road, Kettering.
5. **Carnelley, JA**, Bankfield, Greetland, Halifax.
6. **Coats, JAH**, Skipness, Argyllshire.
7. **Crawford, RF**, 31 Wellington Road, Dublin.
8. **Davids, H**, Windyhill, Kilmalcolm.
9. **Gibson, CS**, 118 West Parade, Hull.
10. **Hogg, CW**, 5 Lothian Road. Middlesborough.
11. **Horne, AW**, Athelstane, Clarence Road, Shanklin.
12. **Humphreys, L**, 5 Mosedale Road, Walton, Liverpool.
13. **James, F**, 13 Plough Terrace, Port Talbot.
14. **Jordan, CR**, 3 Gordon Terrace, Middlesborough.
15. **Lewis, J**, Wilcott, Nesscliff, Shrewsbury.
16. **Mountford, W**, 129 Sweetman Street, Wilverhampton.
17. **Newton, T**, 15 Clifton Street, Wigan.
18. **Oakley, J**, 44 Cambria Street, South Hylton, Sunderland.
19. **Osborn, MA**, 14 Clifton Avenue, Dollis Park, Finchley.
20. **Page, AE**, 2 Vernon Villas, Upper Vernon Road, Sutton, Surrey.
21. **Piper, RA**, 57 Rugby Road, Brighton.
22. **Purves, TW**, Hazelcliffe, Bearsden, Glasgow.
23. **Rawson, RR**, Durdens Lodge, Epsom.
24. **Read, R**, 36 Buckingham Gate, WW.
25. **Sedgley, LE**, 'Rona', Thames Street, Walton-on-Thames.
26. **Sharp, H**, 26 Exeter Street, Derby.
27. **Shields, F**, City YMCA, Belfast.
28. **Thompson, CJM**, Vicarage, Northallerton.
29. **Thompson, H**, 6 Sidney Street, St. Helens, Lancashire.
30. **Watson, FD**, Crummock Park, Beith.

 The number in millions of different combinations you can make from six eight stud LEGO bricks; something a Scout wouldn't have time to know

NIGHTS AWAY

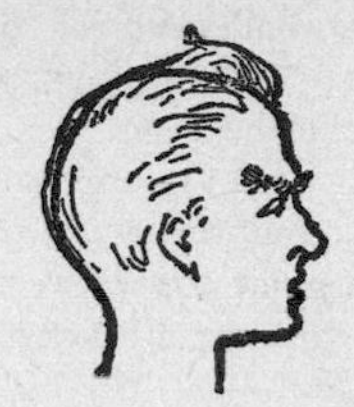

Jerry's first Scout camp didn't just put hairs on his chest.

CRACK THE CODE

Can you work out the Morse code message below, without cheating by using the reference on page 39?

--. .. -. --. / --. .- -. --. / --. --- --- .-.. .. .

Clue: Bit of a watcha.

Answer on page 153.

THE BLACK BEAUTY CONNECTION

A delve into the Scout archives at Gilwell Park reveals a wealth of objects and information. Much of it was produced by B-P himself, as a hugely prolific writer and artist; but one room is almost dedicated to those items that were made to commemorate B-P's success in Mafeking, items given to him as a gesture of thanks or goodwill, or items collected by him to mark moments in his life.

Among these objects there is a carefully mounted horse's hoof. A few enquiries reveals that this is indeed no ordinary hoof, but that of the horse with connections to the classic children's tale *Black Beauty*. The horse, Black Prince, was a gift from the Australian people to Baden-Powell in 1900 after the Siege of Mafeking. It was borrowed by Lucy Kemp-Welch, an artist, who had been commissioned to produce the illustrations for the first illustrated edition of Anna Sewell's *Black Beauty*.

Number of Maltese Scouts who represented their Association at the celebrations for the coronation of King George VI in London in 1937

FIRST WORLD JAM

Sandwiched between the two World Wars, the 1st World Scout Jamboree took place at Olympia, London, in 1920 and gave the general public a chance to see what Scouting was all about. The countries that took part were:

Australia
Belgium
Ceylon (now Sri Lanka)
Chile
China
Czechoslovakia
Denmark
England
Estonia
France
Gibraltar
Greece
India
Ireland
Italy
Jamaica
Japan
Luxembourg
Malaya
Malta
The Netherlands
New Zealand
Norway
Portugal
Romania
Scotland
Serbia
Siam (now Thailand)
South Africa
Spain
Sweden
Switzerland
USA
Wales

NOTES FROM THE FOUNDER

B-P on how to get the right girl...

The right girl will come along sooner or later – if you have kept your head. Your calf-love will have disappeared. You will find a girl whose character you admire and respect, whose tastes are like your own and whose comradeship you long for. It will not be merely her person that attracts you, but her personality.

You will find a new, calmer and deeper form of love that links and binds you to her – one which, if you are wise, will never grow less.

And you will expect her to come to you pure and clean, won't you? But what about yourself? Are you going to expect of her what you cannot offer in return yourself?

That would be neither manly nor fair. No, if you are going to enjoy real happiness in life that is the supreme joy of being married to a really good woman from whom you hope for love and respect, don't begin your married life with a lie, else you will be lying all through it, and there will be an end to trusting each other.

Robert Baden-Powell, *Rovering to Success: A Book of Life-Sport for Young Men*, 1930

 The number in thousands of Cub Scouts in 1923 – the first time they top the 100,000 mark (compared with 85,154 in 1922)

PROVE YOUR PROFICIENCY

Bagging a Boy Scouts Proficiency Badge circa 1909 could be harder than you think.

To wear a **Leatherworker** Badge, you must be able to:

- Sole and heel a pair of boots, repair traces and stirrup leathers and straps
- Dress a saddle or a pair of top boots
- Have a knowledge of tanning and curing, and the parts of a harness

QUOTE UNQUOTE

Without a Scouting background, it would have been more difficult for me to survive some of my adventures.
It got me away from my desk and outside.
Sir Richard Branson,
entrepreneur, adventurer and former Scout

IF YOU LEARN ONE SONG... 'GING GANG GOOLIE'

The song that will no doubt be forever associated with Scouting:

Ging gang goolie goolie goolie goolie watcha,
Ging gang goo, ging gang goo.
Ging gang goolie goolie goolie goolie watcha,
Ging gang goo, ging gang goo.
Hayla, oh hayla shayla, hayla shayla, shayla, oh-ho,
Hayla, oh hayla shayla, hayla shayla, shayla, oh.
Shally wally, shally wally, shally wally, shally wally,
Oompah, oompah, oompah, oompah.

Directions for use in five easy steps:

1. Typically sung as a two-part round, the first verse sung throughout by all.
2. At the end, the first group should keep repeating 'Oompah' while the second group starts again.
3. When the second group reaches 'Hayla' the first group should join in again from this point.
4. At the end of the verse, the group splits once again, but switches parts.
5. The third verse ends abruptly for all at the 'Oom' of the first 'Oompah'.

The number of times Scouting was featured in the British radio, press and online in the first week of 2007

SCOUTS FOR PEACE: MACEDONIA

Scouting isn't just one big carefree Jamboree. With its inclusive approach to all nations, countries and cultures, the Scout Movement has helped many people in war-torn countries over the years, some of which were described in *Scouting* magazine, July 2000...

As the national commissioner of Sojuz Na Izvidnici Na Makedonija (SIM), The Scout Association of the former Yugoslav Republic of Macedonia, Tase felt he had to do something to help people communicate beyond their communities and cultural barriers to try and keep further fighting at bay. He proposed an electronic network and the opening of a computer centre in Skopje. This would operate as a cyber café in the morning, and as a training centre in intercultural learning and creativity in the afternoon. The centre would be designed as a place where young people could meet each other and hopefully build links between the 12 main towns in Macedonia.

WHAT GOES AROUND COMES AROUND

When the Australian Rover Scouts heard about the Centenary Scout initiative, Gifts for Peace, they instantly knew how they were going to spread the word, Aussie-style – with a peace boomerang. Inspired by the traditional Aboriginal wooden ceremonial tool that returns to the person who throws it, they sent this fitting symbol on a tour of Australia that would take in a distance of 18,000km. OK, so the boomerang was not actually thrown – although that would have meant yet another world record for the Scouts! The Scouts did, however, send logbooks with their boomerang, allowing people to write their thoughts on peace, and share their photographs and stories of the adventures it had while in their care. Thankfully the boomerang was spared from any cheeky moments of bad taste – it is a peace boomerang after all. Instead it managed to visit the governor general of Australia, past governor general of Australia, their majesties the King and Queen of Sweden (who must have been around at the time), parliamentarians and councillors, plus Scouts of every section of Australia as well as the general public. After such a long journey, the boomerang finally made it home on 11 July 2006, tired but definitely never peaced-out. Who knows where it might turn up next, spreading its message far and wide.

 Number of films, TV programmes and shorts in which former Scout and actor Henry Fonda appeared between 1935 and 1981

WHOSE BADGE IS IT ANYWAY?

You might have a full arm of new badges. Or you may be taking a trip down memory lane. But can you guess what this Cub Scout Proficiency Badge is for?

a) Pirate
b) *Blue Peter* presenter
c) Boatswain

Answer on page 153.

RIGHT UP THE FOUNDER'S STREET

Baden-Powell has got it covered as far as streets named after him in the UK go. Here are just a few places where you can walk on, or even live in, his namesake:

- Baden-Powell Avenue, *Chesterfield, Derbyshire, S40*
- Baden-Powell Close, *Dagenham, Essex, RM9*
- Baden-Powell Close, *Rugeley, Staffordshire, WS15*
- Baden-Powell Close, *Surbiton, Surrey, KT6*
- Baden-Powell Crescent, *Pontefract, West Yorkshire, WF8*
- Baden-Powell Crescent, *Towcester, Northamptonshire, NN12*
- Baden-Powell Drive, *Colchester, CO3*
- Baden-Powell Road, *Chesterfield, Derbyshire, S40*
- Baden-Powell Road, *Kirkton Industrial Estate, Arbroath, Angus, DD11*
- Baden-Powell Road, *Nottingham, NG2*
- Baden-Powell Road, *Sevenoaks, Kent, TN13*
- Baden-Powell Road, *Turriff, Aberdeenshire, AB53*
- Baden-Powell Street, *Gateshead, Tyne and Wear, NE9*
- Baden-Powell Street, *Walney, Barrow-in-Furness, Cumbria, LA14*
- Baden-Powell Walk, *Kesgrave, Ipswich, IP5*
- Baden-Powell Way, *Romsey, Hampshire, SO51*

Number of Scouts who made their Scout Promise in 1924 to become the first Scouts in Suriname (formerly Nederlands Guyana) near Brazil

QUOTE UNQUOTE

Every Scout has to begin as a tenderfoot and to make a few mistakes at first. As Napoleon said, "A man who never made mistakes never made anything".
Robert Baden-Powell in *Yarns for Boy Scouts* (1909)

BEADS OF SCOUT

Look very carefully at any Scout Leader worth their clout over the last 100 years, and you'll notice two small wooden beads hanging from their coat button-hole or in most part strung on a leather thong or bootlace around the neck. What might look like an innocent toggle (not to be confused with woggle) is in fact proud recognition of an adult who has completed his or her Leadership training. The first Wood Badges, as they are called, were made from beads taken from a grand necklace that had belonged to a Zulu chief named Dinizulu. B-P fought this chief during the Boer war, after Dinizulu raised a rebellion of Zulu tribes following the British break-up of the Zulu kingdom. On state occasions, Dinizulu was known to wear such a necklace that was 12 feet long, containing approximately 1,000 beads made from South African acacia yellow wood. The soft central pith of this wood made it ideal for threading a rawhide lace through and so this is how the 1,000 beads were arranged. Each bead varied in size from tiny emblems to some four inches in length. A necklace of this standing was considered sacred, being the badge conferred on royalty and outstanding warriors. Then according to Scout lore, B-P found the necklace during his time in Zululand in 1888 after he entered a hut that had recently been occupied by Chief Dinizulu. He recognised the beads from a photograph of the chief he happened to have on his person. In his personal notes he speaks of the chief as being 'full of resources, energy and pluck' and when looking for something to commemorate his own outstanding Scouts with, he remembered this respect and the beads. He removed two of the smaller beads, drilled through the centre and threaded them carefully onto a new thong. This would be the very first Wood Badge. All subsequent badges were made from the beads until they began to run short. So what now? Determined not to end the tradition, B-P told the next lot of successful Leaders that they would receive one acacia bead from the necklace and they must carve the other one themselves from hornbeam or beech trees at Gilwell. Eventually Gilwell beech wood beads became the norm and for many years, were whittled by Gilwell staff in their spare time.

108 *Area in acres of ground at Gilwell Park on which Scouts can enjoy camping and other outdoor activities*

CELEBRITY SCOUTS: NEIL ARMSTRONG

What this famous Scout did next...

The man who made the famous 'giant leap for mankind' has more than the memory of crunching on lunar craters in common with his fellow US moonwalkers. According to www.boyscouttrail.com (a site for Boy Scouts of America) 11 of the 12 American astronauts who have walked on the moon were also Scouts – including Neil Armstrong's fellow *Apollo 11* passengers Edwin 'Buzz' Aldrin and Michael Collins. Of the 21 astronauts who have orbited the moon, 19 have been Scouts, while 142 of America's 214 former and present astronauts have also taken part in Scouting. Born 5 August 1930, Armstrong was a test pilot and naval aviator whose first space flight was as command pilot of *Gemini 8* in 1966. His last and most historic space voyage was as mission commander of *Apollo 11*, which landed on the moon on 20 July 1969. The lunar crater 'Armstrong', located 50km away from the spacecraft, was subsequently named in his honour. But this was not the first of Armstrong's accolades. The ambitious astronaut-to-be spent most of his youth rising through the ranks of the Boy Scouts, finally earning the distinguished Eagle Scout Award and the Silver Buffalo Award.

One legend goes that a fledgling desire to walk on the moon was in fact triggered by a vision of the moon through the telescope of amateur astronomer Jacob Zint, while at Scout camp with Boy Scout Troop 14. The first words Armstrong spoke to mission control upon landing *Apollo* on the moon, were: 'Houston, tranquillity base here. The Eagle has landed.' In fact two Eagles had landed – spacecraft *Apollo 11* and Eagle Scout Armstrong. He now lives in happy retirement with his wife in Ohio.

NOTES FROM THE FOUNDER

B-P on Gilwell...

In 1919, Mr De Bois Maclaren presented to our association the estate of Gilwell Park, adjoining Epping Forest. His idea was to provide a camping ground within easy reach of London for the poorer class of boy but, seeing that there were suitable buildings on the estate he consented to my suggestion that we should make it also the Training School for Scoutmasters, which I looked upon as an all important step in the development of the Movement.

Lord Baden-Powell of Gilwell,
***Lessons from the Varsity of Life*, 1933**

Number of Scouting countries that took part in the JOTA – Jamboree on the Air – in 2001; this event connects Scouts from all over the world, by radio 109

COME ON, LIGHT MY FIRE

Athens in 2004 was a very excitable and busy place, thanks to the Olympic Games. As is customary, the Olympic torch was carried into the arena on the opening day – this year Friday 13 August – where it would relight the Olympic flame to mark the end of its momentous relay around the globe. In 2004 the torch was carried on its final steps by Dr Marie-Louise Correa, Chairman of the World Scout Committee and the first woman and black African to ever hold the post. The torch had exchanged hands more than 11,000 times. The moment was a proud one for the Scouts who had also come up with the concept of an Olympic Truce, to be called at this time. The Truce, which calls for world peace, was backed by the World Organisation of the Scout Movement, the World Association of Girl Guides and Girl Scouts (together making a total of 38 million boys and girls), the United Nations and some 160 countries and states. If only world peace could be found before the next Olympics...

COLLECTOR'S PARADISE

The kind of Scouting treats you might find on auction site eBay, along with their starting prices:

World Girl Guides/Brownie metal pin badge................. £0.99
Pair of Thailand Girl Guide epaulettes £0.99
Hong Kong Girl Guide Association badge £0.75
19th World Scout Jamboree Albania badge £0.99
2005 EuroJam Scout Jamboree Lake Geneva Subcamp badge... £0.99
20th World Scout Jamboree 2003 UK contingent pin badge £0.99
20th World Scout Jamboree Thailand 2003 Join In badge...... £6.00
BSA National Jamboree 2005 backpatch and badge........... £2.20
Centenary of Scouting 2007 woven Scout badge £0.75
30 x Hong Kong Scout district badges – some rare £14.99
12-language 2007 World Scout Jamboree/Centenary badges £9.99
Chile Scouting 75th Anniversary Scout badge................ £0.75
Five Scout badges – 2005 EuroJam Jamboree badges.......... £2.45
20th World Scout Jamboree official leather woggle £1.65
20th World Scout Jamboree official badge £2.45
Set of Mongolia Boy Scout progress award badges............ £2.48
Colombia Scout membership and strip badge................ £0.99
World Scouting – Afghanistan Scout membership badge £0.99
Ghana Scout Association membership ribbon badge £0.99

 Cost in pounds for the use of 14 braziers (containers in which to make fire) at Youlbury Scout Activity Centre, until 2008

SCOUTS OF THE WORLD: ERADICATING POLIO IN ANGOLA

Keeping the Scout Promise to 'help others'...

Angola is one of only eight countries in the world where the wild polio virus is still present. Many children are victim of this virus, which attacks the nervous system and provokes paralysis. One Scout, named Celso, thought that he might be able to help by encouraging other young people top take ownership of social change. In partnership with UNICEF, he promoted the Angola Scout Association to organise an immunisation campaign all over the country, to try and eradicate polio. More than 5,000 Scouts from various groups across the country worked in teams to take the immunisation messages to more than 200,000 houses and marketplaces where mothers would meet. As a result over one million people got the message. Scouts also spread the news at international football matches at the National Stadium and through megaphone rallies and street theatres in schools and public places. Every year, more Scouts take part in the initiative and the results are coming through. According to UNICEF, in 2004, 96% of the five million children targeted to receive polio immunisation did so at National Immunisation Days. The country is now well on the way to being absolutely free from polio.

QUOTE UNQUOTE

We had to virtually live off the land... we caught rabbits and hedgehogs... we learnt to tickle trout. It really made David Bellamy what David Bellamy became – someone who is totally empassioned about wildlife and the farming element of wildlife.

David Bellamy, naturalist and former Scout

MISSING SCOUT

Currently there are only six countries without Scouting. They are:

- Andorra
- Cuba
- Democratic People's Republic of Korea (North Korea)
- Myanmar (Burma)
- People's Democratic Republic of Laos
- People's Republic of China

Number of the Commonwealth Act that gave the Boy Scouts of the Philippines or Kapatirang Scouting ng Pilipinas their official status in 1936

AN A-Z OF ACTIVITY BADGES: N-Q

This most up-to-date list of Scout Activity Badges proves there's more than one reason to join the Scouts. The list is provided in bite-sized pieces throughout the book so as not to get badge addicts too over-excited.

- Naturalist
- Nights away (staged)
- Basic Nautical Skills
- Nautical Skills
- Advanced Nautical Skills
- Navigator
- Orienteer
- Parascending
- Photographer
- Physical Recreation
- Pioneer
- Power Coxswain
- Public Relations
- Pulling
- Quartermaster

NIGHTS AWAY

That was the point at which Nigel realised he'd got the slip knot wrong.

 Number of UK Scouts who attended the 10th World Scout Jamboree in Laguna, Philippines, in 1959 – the first in Asia

WHAT A JAMBOREE!

The Jamboree has been a feature of Scouting since 1920 and will feature prominently in 2007 for Scouting's Centenary. But what does the word 'jamboree' mean? Here are a few points of view, as published in *The Scouter*, August 1920...

'Joy to every Scout today
As from the lands after they throng,
Meeting here for work and play.
Be prepared, the Scouts' own song,
Over countless miles has gone,
Ringing through our boyhood world;
Ever may their song go on,
Ever be their flag unfurled!'
– Evening News

'The word "jamboree" does not seem, as one might imagine, to be derived from the Australian backwoods. The dictionaries explain it vaguely as "American slang"; and the first appearance of it in print seems to be in *Scribner's Magazine* for 1872. It usually occurs in a festive and even disreputable, connection; and the Boy Scouts' revel may be considered as marking a stage in its progress towards respectability.'
– The Observer

'It is a merry word. One may say confidently, without knowing what the verb means exactly, that all properly constituted boys ought to jamboree. Perhaps it may be defined as 'playing the wise fool'. The first Boy Scouts were town boys, taught, to their intense joy and surprise, country arts and amusements; and the Movement has grown above others because it has the breath of the open air in it, and most admirably corrects the urban mentality of the young generation.' *– Daily Mail*

'"Jamboree", the name by which the Boy Scouts' gathering at Olympia is known, has a fine sounding ring about it that will surely before long find echo in hundreds of celebrations up and down the country. We have a habit in England of naming our festive occasions from foreign sources. We have our soirées and conversaziones, whose meanings have puzzled few since the days of Sam Weller. There is our old friends the gymkhana, which the *Oxford Dictionary* tells us is a "mixture of gym (nastics) and (Hindustani) *gend-khana*, ballhouse, racquet court". What school sports were formerly complete without the dak-race? We have since learned to call it a relay race–dak meaning in India simply post or transport by relays. But as we take our terms of amusement from other tongues, so the French came to us for their sporting expressions – *le boxe*, "football", and the rest.' *– Manchester Guardian*

Number of UK Scout Counties and Areas in the Census of Membership of the United Kingdom in 2001 113

THE CAMP COOK: FISH IN NEWSPAPER

From *Backwoods Cooking – Practical Methods and Recipes*, a reprint of a popular collection that first appeared in *Scouting* magazine.

You will need:

- One fish per person
- Greaseproof paper
- Newspaper
- String

Method:

1. Prepare the fish, removing the innards, and place on a sheet of greaseproof paper, which is folded to completely surround the fish.
2. Take six sheets of (tabloid) newspaper and make up a parcel with the fish in the centre, tying it all up securely with string.
3. Place the parcel in a bowl of water until the paper is soaked through.
4. Remove the package from the water and squeeze excess water out gently.
5. Place the damp parcel on hot embers, turning every five minutes. The fish should be cooked by the time the paper begins to char.

SCOUT'S HORROR: THE DEVIL DOGS

No *Scout's Companion* would be complete without a few Scouting horror stories, sad yarns, odd tales and wicked deeds, just to balance the books. The tellers of these anecdotes wish to remain anonymous just in case the Scouts come and make them do some good turns.

'One particular Scout camp I remember would back on to a forest. Perfect for some *Blair Witch Project*-type stuff. We would pull some red cat's-eyes up from the road and push them in pairs into the ground, or stick them into the bark of trees on the edge of the forest. After dinner we would sit around the fire and tell the younger kids the legend of the 'devil dogs'. We'd say there was a Cub that fell victim to them when he slept with his head outside the tent, and that his friends didn't realise until they pulled in his headless body. We would mention that you used to be able to see their red eyes glowing after midnight, and then leave them to it. A little while later, come back and snap some branches in the woods behind the tent, out come the torches, cat's-eyes reflect and, voila, instant requests for "mummy".' **A Photographer**

 Door number, from and to number 116, of the first Scout Headquarters on Victoria Street, London, SW1

GETTING LYRICAL

Scouts take their place in the music Hall of Fame...

Fatboy Slim –
'Weapon Of Choice'
'As I drift off into the night, I'm in flight,
She's a Boy Scout, no doubt'

Peter Gabriel –
'San Jacinto'
'Follow dry river bed – watch Scout and Guides make
pow-wow signs.'

Son of Dork –
'Slacker'
'Eats low-carb ice-cream with his mum,
Sews Cub Scout badges on his sweater.'

Bette Midler –
'You'll Never Get Away from Me'
'I warn you that I'm no Boy Scout.
Relax awhile, come dance with me.'

Stereophonics –
'A Thousand Trees'
'Where the matchstick men are made,
At the Scouts' hall'

THREE LAWS LATER

Baden-Powell set up the Wolf Cubs in 1916. They were renamed Cub Scouts in 1966. In 1991, girls were allowed to join the Pack. For each change, the law was amended to fit the times...

The original laws of the Wolf Cub Pack
The Cub gives in to the Old Wolf.
The Cub does not give in to himself.

The original Cub Scout law
A Cub Scout always does his best,
thinks of others before himself, and does a good turn every day.

The amended Cub Scout law
Cub Scouts always do their best,
think of others before themselves, and do a good turn every day.

AIN'T NO MOUNTAIN HIGH ENOUGH

Some Scouts love to ramble, and none so much as little Cub Scout Jordan Ross. In 2006, he completed a marathon hill-walking challenge that had taken him five years. In November 2006, he was still only nine years and seven months old. The challenge he set himself was to climb all of the 'Wainwright' hills in the Lake District – 214 of them as defined by Alfred Wainwright's celebrated guidebooks to the area. Of these 214 'hills' some of them are the highest mountains in England. Jordan first got the Wainwright bug when he was four years old, hiking up Catbells. His final hill was Castle Crag. All walks were scheduled to fit into the school holidays so as not to disrupt his education. But Jordan still found time to climb Snowdon and Ben Nevis as well. His parents are currently trying to dissuade him from climbing Everest until he is perhaps a little bit older.

CRACK THE CODE

Can you work out the Morse code message below, without cheating by using the reference on page 39?

--. .. .-.. .-- . .-.. .-.. / .--. .- .-. -.-

Clue: A Baron place.

Answer on page 153.

THINGS ALL SCOUTS SHOULD KNOW

In everyday life, both in town and country, there are interesting 'signs' to test your scoutcraft...
from *The Scout*, No 1, Volume I, 15 August 1908

Squeaking boots

It is very annoying to find that your boots squeak when you are engaged on a particular piece of tracking. Squeaking boots can be easily cured in this way:

From your shoemaker get two wooden pegs. Having made a small hole in the centre of each boot, drive the pegs home. After this you will find that your boots squeak no more.

This is a very much better plan than standing the boot in oil for a more or less lengthy period, the method which is usually suggested, for the oil not only discolours the boot, but makes it almost impossible to polish it for weeks afterwards.

 Longitude number of degrees east for Beijing, China – something all Scouts trying to navigate their way there should know

NIGHTS AWAY

Cedric so desperately wanted to be in the Peewit Patrol. Like a true songbird, he practised the call night and day.

QUOTE UNQUOTE

'I have spent more time out in the wild than most people. Scouting has certainly helped.'
Sir David Attenborough, wildlife presenter and former Scout

NOTES FROM THE FOUNDER

B-P on stalking with a camera...

Big game Kodak-ing is taking the place of big game shooting, as the recognised form of sport. Where big game hunters used to compare notes over their rifles they now do so with no less interest over their cameras. It implies more crafty stalking and as great daring and skill as ever. The trophies, especially if gained with a movie camera, form a far more exciting record both for yourself and for your friends than any dead horns and hides.

It is tending to make the big game hunter more of a naturalist than a butcher, and it leaves fauna still intact for our sons to hunt in their turn, in the same fashion, and so to learn the invaluable lesson one gains in the school of the jungle.

Robert Baden-Powell,
***Lessons from the Varsity of Life*, 1933**

ON TOP OF THE WORLD

On 17 May 2006, Rhys Jones, a Scout Network member from Hampshire, was getting really high. This was the day he reached the summit of Everest and, in doing so, became the youngest ever person to climb all seven of the highest peaks on each of the world's continents (specified as North America, South America, Antarctica, Europe, Africa, Australia and Asia). It was also the date of his 20th birthday. Already a record-breaking mountaineer, he is also the youngest Briton to have successfully climbed Alaska's 20,232ft Mount McKinley, and the youngest to summit Mount Vinson – the highest mountain in Antarctica. On reaching the top of Everest he joined only 10 other Britons who have managed to climb the highest peaks on each of the world's seven continents, and one of only 100 people in the world who had completed this feat. In case any other Scouts wish to follow in his footsteps, the full list of the seven peaks Rhys climbed are:

Mount McKinley *North America*
Mount Aconcagua *South America*
Mount Kilimanjaro *Africa*
Mount Kosciusko *Australia*
Mount Elbrus *Europe*
Mount Vinson *Antarctica*
Mount Everest *Asia*

REASONS FOR THE INSTITUTIONS OF GIRL GUIDES

'The Scheme For Girl Guides'*, as published in the *Headquarters Gazette*, July 1909 to December 1910...

Decadence is going on in the nation, both moral and physical: proofs are only too plentiful. It is preventable if taken in time. Much of this decadence is due to ignorance or supineness of mothers who have never been taught themselves.

Physical defects exist to an enormous extent, a large proportion of which are preventable.

Moral education is left by the mothers pretty much to the schoolmaster.

Girls must be partners and comrades rather than dolls. Their influence in after life on the actions and quality of the men is very great; they become their 'guides'. They therefore need character training quite as much as boys.

** This rough and incomplete outline is intended in answer to numerous enquiries. The 'scheme' may be obtained after 16 November from headquarters, price 3d.*

118 *Number of Scout Associations at the International symposium on 'Scouting: Youth without Borders, Partnership and Solidarity', in 1994*

SCOUTS FOR PEACE: YUGOSLAVIA

Scouting isn't just one big carefree Jamboree. With its inclusive approach to all nations, countries and cultures, the Scout Movement has helped many people in war-torn countries over the years, some of which were described in *Scouting* magazine, July 2000...

In 2000, Nikola was 15 years old and a Patrol Leader in the Serbian branch of the Yugoslav Scout Association. During the war, he and his patrol worked alongside the Red Cross, undertaking civil defence responsibilities. Together with other Scouts, he helped to rescue the victims of the bombings, to evacuate children and old people and to clear bomb sites. He also helped to organise activities in the air raid shelters and recreational activities for all young people. His greatest wish is to develop contacts and exchanges with other young people of his own age throughout Europe, something that the international Scout network helped him to do. In this way, he hopes that an alternative way of resolving conflict can be found as opposed to violence.

SCOUTS OF THE WORLD: ROMA SCOUTS IN SLOVAKIA

Keeping the Scout Promise to 'help others'...

The Roma community (often referred to as 'gypsies') is frowned upon in many European countries, due in part to their nomadic and exotic culture. In many countries it is often the most marginalised minority. Out of five and a half million people living in Slovakia, the Romas make up half a million of the population. Poverty is widespread and many of them live in ghettos. As often happens, the children are affected most, living in poor and unhealthy conditions, with no access to education or hope for the future. But by making contact with the Slovak Scout Association, one group of Roma youths has been able to try and transform their community. From an initial Club of Right Roma Boys and Girls, they became the first Roma Scouts. They then developed an education programme designed to meet the needs of Roma children and youths, while Leaders received training to help them implement new initiatives. Roma Scouting retained its own symbols, uniform, badges, flags and hymn. However, their welcome into the Scouts has encouraged a more tolerant acceptance of their community from non-Romas.

Number of Scouts who were named Scout of the Year in Hong Kong between 1987 and 2005

PATROL NAMES AND THEIR PECULIARITIES: THE WOODPECKER

As referred to in an enlightening series by JR Stanley (author of *Five Boys and a Master*) in *The Scouter*, January 1930:

- The woodpecker's mysterious whistling 'yaffle' is often heard, and his curious flight betrays him.
- The pecker's peculiar laughing cry is often heard when rain is near, and in some districts he is called the 'rainbird'.
- Woodpeckers are characterised by straight bills of moderate length and thickness, well adapted for chiselling into wood.
- A woodpecker's foot has the outer front toe turned back so that the toes are in pairs, which is useful for holding onto tree trunks.
- The starling, often upsets the pecker's domestic arrangements.
- The pecker's remarkable tongue, a silvery-looking instrument several inches in length, coated with a sticky mucus, picks up the insects and their larvae with great rapidity.
- The woodpecker is therefore a real Scout bird – a friend of the farmer and forester.
- If pursued by a hawk, the pecker darts for the trees for shelter, where he plays the game of hide and seek with his pursuer.
- The cry of the green woodpecker, given as 'heearfle-arfle-arfa', conveys little and must be learned from the bird itself.

JIM FIXED IT FOR US

An over-excited Pack of Cub Scouts cramming their faces with buns and slurping pop on a Blackpool rollercoaster might not be most people's idea of primetime TV viewing, but when Jimmy Savile 'fixed it' for the Cubs of 2nd Sutton-in-Ashfield to do just that, it was a sight that many people will never forget. For some it is the image that springs to mind first when they think of the Cubs and was inspiration to write to *Jim'll Fix It* themselves.

But the stomach-churning exercise was neither regulation Cub practice, an act of childish bravado, nor simply a silly stunt for the cameras. Along with their giant *Jim'll Fix It* badge – big enough to surround the whole Cub Pack – the programme prompted the people of Sutton-in-Ashfield to raise £477 for Jimmy Savile's Stoke Mandeville Hospital Appeal.

Cub Scout Leader Tony Miller would also sleep soundly at night in the knowledge that staff at the BBC thought his Pack had produced the funniest 'fix-it' ever.

 Cost in pounds for the use of 18 dens (meeting areas) at Youlbury Scout Activity Centre, until 2008

THINGS ALL SCOUTS SHOULD KNOW

In everyday life, both in town and country, there are interesting 'signs' to test your scoutcraft...
from *The Scout*, No 1, Volume I, 21 June 1908

Seen on macs

Many people who possess mackintoshes probably never use the small band which is attached to the cuffs of the garment. They seem to smarten up the general appearance certainly, but, as perhaps few are aware, they have a use as well. In wet and windy weather it is so much more comfortable to have the sleeves folded round and buttoned up as in the second small sketch – indeed it becomes almost a necessity if the wearer is cycling, and the band, of course, makes this a simple matter.

QUOTE UNQUOTE

I don't mind confessing that I have a weakness for hippos.
Robert Baden-Powell,
Lessons from the Varsity of Life, 1933

DEAR BADEN-POWELL...

Even as early as 1908, Baden-Powell recognised the potential power of the problem page and set about answering his fellow Scouts' questions with suitable aplomb...

Tea-drinking

E Clark, of Bristol, is anxious to know whether I would advise Scouts to give up tea-drinking. No, I should not. Tea is a refreshing beverage and if properly made, not harmful. But it should be drunk within five minutes of making, for if tea is allowed to 'stew' it is very injurious indeed. The Australian bushmen – who are real Scouts – consume large quantities of tea. Their method of making it is very primitive, and consists of putting a handful of tea into their billie, and drinking it without sugar or milk; and a very good drink it is too. And after a hard day's work in the bush, perhaps there is no greater pleasure for the 'men of the wild' than to fortify themselves with the cup that cheers. I think it is generally admitted by medical authorities that tea made properly and consumed moderately is not only an exceedingly refreshing beverage, but also has a beneficial effect upon the system. So, E Clark of Bristol can still follow in the footsteps of the great Scout pioneers and take this modest cup of tea. But, while I recommend tea as a beverage, it should not be taken in excess, nor too strong. But this is a danger not likely to occur to the Scouts, as their special training teaches them moderation.

'Round the Campfire' in *The Scout*, No 1, Volume I, 18 April 1908

CELEBRITY SCOUTS: SIR DAVID ATTENBOROUGH

What this famous Scout did next...

You could say that bringing nature to the nation is something of a specialty for the man who famously whispered: 'There is more meaning and mutual understanding in exchanging a glance with a gorilla than any other animal I know.' This seminal moment was watched by 500 million people worldwide in his landmark series *Life on Earth* in 1974.

It all began in 1952 when David Attenborough joined BBC Television's talks department, launching the first of his famous *Zoo Quest* series two years later. For the past 50 years, Sir David has been taking us on a journey to some of the wildest spots on Earth, culminating in his most recent and yet more extraordinary series, *Planet Earth*. Although now officially an octogenarian – he turned 80 in 2006 – his quest for nature shows no sign of slowing down. Fans can look forward to his next series, *Life in Cold Blood*, in 2008. For all this, and much, much more, Sir David was awarded the Order of Merit by the Queen in 2005. In terms of Scout Proficiency Badges, where do we begin? Explorer, Guide, Hillwalker, Meteorology, Naturalist, Orienteer, Pioneer, Observer, Photography, Survival Skills, World Conservation and World Friendship Badges seem to have been designed in his honour. A true leader of the pack.

QUOTE UNQUOTE

You will sleep all the better when bedtime comes if you have been busy through the day.

Robert Baden-Powell on 'The Joy of the Open Road' in *Rovering to Success – A Book of Life-sport for Young Men*, 1930

PROVE YOUR PROFICIENCY

Bagging a Boy Scouts Proficiency Badge circa 1909 could be harder than you think.

To wear a **Plumber** Badge, you must be able to...

- Make wiped and brazed joints
- Cut and fix a window pane
- Repair a burst pipe
- Mend a ball fence tap
- Understand the ordinary hot and cold water system of a house

 The minimum number in metres that Scouts have to drive their built electric slot car racer as part of the Model Maker Activity Badge

NOTES FROM THE FOUNDER

B-P on the motto...

The slogan of the Scout is 'be prepared'. This was adopted, with much of the uniform, from the South African constabulary. The men of the force chose that motto for themselves partly because it spoke to their readiness to take on any kind of duty at any time, and also because it brought in my initials.

Robert Baden-Powell, *Lessons from the Varsity of Life*, 1933

GIFTS FOR PEACE

In 2006 the Saudi king, called for the World Organisation of the Scout Movement to encourage all 28 million Scouts to join the Gifts for Peace programme. This was designed as part of Centenary celebrations, where each Scout Association in the world was asked to come with a Gift for Peace to show how they were continuing to work for peace. Speaking in Ridyadh, he said: 'The God of Judaism, the God of Islam and the God of Christianity are the same God. We just pray to him in different ways, so we should all be working to make this a more peaceful world.' Raising his hand in the Scout sign, he saluted the young people of the world and pledged his support for their work. King Abdullah is recognised as the inspiration behind the Gifts for Peace programme and also pledged initial funding. The programme so far involves Scouts in 70 countries. The UK Scout's three Key Gifts, at national level, are:

Creating a more peaceful world
'We will refine our Member Programme to include greater focus on personal values and peace, emphasising the promise and law. This will ensure that our programme remains relevant to young people. We will work with others to devise appropriate educational methods.'

Encouraging greater solidarity
'We will build upon our international contacts and networks and encourage more young people to form partnerships with Scout communities across the world, using as a basis the Marrakech Charter. We will also improve our sharing of such experiences throughout our Association.'

Challenging prejudice
'We will widen the diversity of our UK membership and reach out to displaced groups and indigenous minority groups. By being more diverse, the Movement will be more relevant to local communities, drawing upon the widest range of views and experiences. This mirrors the aim of Scouting in providing opportunities for all young people in our communities.'

Approximate number in thousands of Scouts in Germany (as at 2005); actual number is 123,937

THINGS ALL SCOUTS SHOULD KNOW

In everyday life, both in town and country, there are interesting 'signs' to test your scoutcraft...
from *The Scout*, No 1, Volume I, 21 May 1908

Instead of cutting corks

After withdrawing a cork from a bottle, the former rapidly expands, and when one wishes to replace it one frequently finds that it had become too large for the purpose. The usual remedy in such cases is to pare pieces off the side. This, however, is seldom satisfactory, for the cork, as a rule, is far from airtight and, in some cases, will not even keep the liquid in. A better way is to place it on the floor and roll it backwards and forwards with one's foot, putting a certain amount of pressure on it.

After a few minutes of this persuasive treatment it will have become fairly soft and can be inserted in the bottle without difficulty.

WHICH WAY NORTH?

Being in control of a compass means knowing a bit more than just your north, east, south and west. A true Scout should know there are three norths to consider for a start...

True north: Each day the Earth rotates about its axis once. The ends of the axis are the true North and true South Poles.

Grid north: The grid lines, pointing to grid north, an Ordnance Survey maps divide great Britain into 100km sections. They are then further sub-divided into 1km squares east of an imaginary zero point in the Atlantic Ocean, west of Cornwall. The majority of grid lines are 1.5 degrees west of true north and are therefore useful lines to refer to when taking bearings.

Magnetic north: A compass needle points to the magnetic North Pole. Unfortunately, it is not in the same position as the true North Pole. The magnetic North Pole is currently located in the Baffin Island region of Canada, and from the United Kingdom, it is west of true north. The difference between grid north and magnetic north is known as the magnetic variation and its value can be found in the orientation panel or margin of an Ordnance Survey map.

As true north is only about 1.5 degrees off grid north, it is so small that it is normally disregarded and only grid north and magnetic north are used.

 Number of 'competing' Scouts from Wales at the 1st World Scout Jamboree in Olympia, London

BADGE TO REALITY

Some badges that would never make it into the Scouts but might give one a better introduction into the mechanics of the modern world:

Adulterer
Binge-Drinker
Computer Games
Fast-Food Lover
Internet Nerd
Litterbug
Manic Text Messager
Media Luvvie
Minor Celebrity
Ozone-Destroyer
Perpetual Bum
Polar Cap-Melter
Raver
Stalker
Tax Dodger
TV Addict
War-Monger
Work-Shirker

QUOTE UNQUOTE

I got my Semaphore badge but have never had much use for it. The Computer Badge seems eminently sensible. I'm surprised there isn't a mobile phone texting badge yet.

Giles Brandreth, broadcaster and former Scout
(quoted in *The Telegraph*, July 2006)

THE CAMP COOK: ACORN COFFEE

From *Backwoods Cooking – Practical Methods and Recipes*, a reprint of a popular collection that first appeared in *Scouting* magazine.

You will need:

- About 40 acorns
- Salt
- Milk and sugar as required
- Water

Method:

1. Wash the acorns well and chop them roughly, using a sharp knife.
2. Place on three sheets of foil, in which you have pierced holes and place over hot embers for about five minutes, shaking regularly.
3. Remove from the fire and allow to cool before chopping the acorns up into smaller pieces and adding to eight cupfuls of boiling water in a foil pan, adding a small pinch of salt to the water.
4. Simmer for three or four minutes and, immediately prior to serving, add a small quantity of cold water to the pan to make the acorn grounds settle.
5. Serve with milk and sugar. *Makes six servings.*

Number in miles of the annual Devizes to Westminster canoe race; in 2005, two Explorer Scouts were the first to complete this race in a number of years

THE RADIOACTIVE SCOUT

According to an article by Ken Silverstein in *Harper's Magazine* (and later published on www.dangerouslaboratories.org), Golf Manor – a small place some 25 miles outside of Detroit – is 'the kind of place where nothing unusual is supposed to happen, where the only thing lurking around the corner is an ice-cream truck.' But on 26 June 1995, the place was swarming with men in white moon suits. They were dismantling a shed and stuffing the pieces into drums emblazoned with radioactive warning signs. The radiation was caused by one David Hahn, a 'gangly', 'ordinary boy' Member of the Scouts. He became known as The Radioactive Boy Scout...

Inspired by a present of *The Golden Book of Chemistry Experiments* David became immersed in science. He soon managed to cause an explosion by making nitroglycerin in his family basement at 12 years.

By 15 years, he was on the road to irradiating anything he could. This was also the year he earned his 'Atomic Energy' badge in the Scouts. (Thank goodness this is not one of the Badges currently on offer from the British Scouts.

By now, his parents had banned his experiments from the family home. But David just shifted his operations to his mother's shed nearby.

He obtained government licensed radioactive materials and knowledge by pretending to be a physics teacher and acquired other vital components from a succession of objects including batteries, lantern mantles, some smoke detectors and a $10 clock.

It was not long before he had managed to make a radium gun from the sum of these parts. But 'real fission' was what David wanted!

So, he followed a schematic in one of his father's books for a model breeder reactor.

Strangely, David's little experiment produced a teeny bit more radioactivity than even he considered safe (he cleverly kept a Geiger counter to hand).

He panicked and tried to hide the evidence in his car. But police responded to a call about a boy stealing tyres and by sheer coincidence found the results of David's project in the boot of his car.

The shed was dismantled. Some 39 barrels of radioactive matter were later trucked to the Great Salt Lake Desert to 'while away' with other debris.

David Hahn is now in the Navy, where among other things, he reads about criminal law. The article relays that he doesn't believe he took more than five years off his life. Thankfully he was stopped before he managed to take the lives of any others.

 Number of the recipe for a 'Scout Barbecue' on www.scoutarama.com; the recipe is actually for a brown hamburger in a bun

NIGHTS AWAY

The Scouts were excitedly discussing the notice. Taking notes was their absolute favourite form of fun – so they might as well start with this one.

QUOTE UNQUOTE

If you just learn a single trick, Scout, you'll get along a lot better with all kinds of folks. You never really understand a person until you consider things from his point of view... Until you climb inside of his skin and walk around in it.

Atticus Finch in *To Kill a Mockingbird* (1962 film version of Harper Lee's book, starring Gregory Peck)

Number of days it took for French Scout, Jean-Michel Chalon, to cycle 9,300km around the Mediterranean 127

100 YEARS OF SCOUTING: 1970s

1970

March	'Bob-a-Job' Week is renamed Scout Job Week in anticipation of decimalisation.
April	Queen's Guides join the annual parade of Queen's Scouts at Windsor Castle.

1971

January	British Scouts begin wearing a new World Membership Badge, a badge worn by Scouts from all over the world.
February	The premiere of a new Scout film, *These Are Scouts*, is attended by Olave, Lady Baden-Powell, the World Chief Guide.

1976

September	Girls are formally allowed to become Venture Scouts after a number experimental schemes have been permitted.
December	Joint Scout and Guide badge is launched to support the Queen's Silver Jubilee appeal.

1977

June	Olave, Lady Baden-Powell, the World Chief Guide, dies aged 88.

NOTES FROM THE FOUNDER

B-P on the value of hide-and-seek...

The game of hide-and-seek is really one of the best games for a boy, and can be elaborated until it becomes Scouting in the field. It teaches you a lot.

I was strongly addicted to it as a child, and the craft learned in that innocent field of sport has stood me in good stead in many a critical time since. To lie flat in a furrow among the currant bushes before the pursuer came in sight taught me the value of not using the most obvious cover, since it would at once be searched. The hunters went at once to the box bushes as the likely spot, while I could watch their doings from among the stems of the currant bushes.

Often I have seen hostile Scouts searching the obvious bits of cover, but they did not find me there...

Robert Baden-Powell, *The Adventures of a Spy*, 1936, first published as *My Adventures as a Spy*, 1915

 Number of Scouts and Leaders attempting a Guinness World Record in the Blue Peter *studios during a Scout edition of the show in February 2007*

BUSH BOOKS

Great books of reference for Rovers, and their prices, as decreed by Robert Baden-Powell in *Rovering to Success: A Book of Life-Sport for Young Men*, 1930

Camping and Woodcraft, Kephart (Macmillan), 10s 6d.
The Gentle Art of Tramping, Stephen Graham (benn), 5s.
Exploring, Gilcraft (Pearson), 2s 6d and 1s 6d.
Camping for All, EE Reynolds (Black), 2s 6d.
Hiking, DF Morgan (Pearson), 1s 6d.

PATROL NAMES AND THEIR PECULIARITIES: THE HAWK

As referred to in an enlightening series by JR Stanley (author of *Five Boys and a Master*) in *The Scouter*, January 1930:

- There are several kinds of hawks, of which the kestrel is the most familiar.
- The kestrel hawk has a habit of suspending himself in mid-air for long periods of time.
- The beak, eyes and claws of the hawk stamp it as a bird of prey.
- The food of a kestrel is mostly obtained from creatures which keep to the ground, such as mice, voles and beetles.
- The sparrow-hawk, which is the patrol bird, is a fine, upstanding, majestic creature with magnificent piercing eyes, a cruel-looking beak and very powerful claws.
- The feet of a hawk have a strong hind-toe set at the same level as the rest and the outer toes are united at the vase by a short web.
- The contracted claw of a hawk's foot forces the sharp nails into the body of its victim; the beak is not used to kill.
- A hawk's nest is a rough platform of sticks in a tall tree.
- A hawk usually lays five bluish-white eggs blotched with red or brown.
- A hen hawk is about the size of a wood pigeon and is larger than the male.
- Sparrow-hawks Scout for their prey in the woods and hedgerows, gliding easily to and fro and finally rushing on their prey at great speed.
- The hawk is too nervous and spiteful for successful use in falconry.
- The Patrol cry of the hawk is 'kreeie', high-pitched, shrill and metallic.

THE CAMP COOK: NETTLE FRITTERS

From *Backwoods Cooking – Practical Methods and Recipes*, a reprint of a popular collection that first appeared in *Scouting* magazine.

You will need:

- A bowl of young nettle leaves
- Two eggs
- Salt, pepper and nutmeg to taste
- A small amount of butter and flour for frying

Method:

1. Blanch the leaves in boiling water for one minute.
2. Rinse the leaves immediately in cold water to preserve the colour.
3. Chop the leaves finely and mix with the beaten eggs.
4. Add salt, pepper and nutmeg to taste.
5. Form portions of the mixture into balls about the size of a golf ball and then flatten into small patties.
6. Dip each of the patties in flour and fry in a foil pan with butter, turning regularly.
7. Serve with rashers of bacon, burgers or other such meats. *Serves two.*

SCOUT'S HORROR: WHY AM I HERE?

No *Scout's Companion* would be complete without a few Scouting nightmares, sad yarns, odd tales and wicked deeds, just to balance the books. The tellers of these anecdotes wish to remain anonymous just in case the Scouts come and make them do some good turns.

'I was in the Cub Scouts for maybe two and a half years in the late 1970s. I remember running away from the first meeting I went to. We were sent off to do some stuff that I didn't understand with some people I didn't know. We were one of three Packs in the town – we were the third but the other two were the eighth and the fifth. I didn't really understand this but accepted it. After the running away episode, I had to go and meet the leader of the Scout Troop to whom our Cub Pack was attached. He asked me lots of questions about Scouting. I didn't know any of the answers. One of the questions was 'who founded the Scouting Movement?' I didn't know. He attempted to prompt me saying it was the same as a famous petrol company. I still didn't know. He meant BP.

'I'd never heard of them either. I'd been living in Brazil so I knew Petrobras, but not British Petroleum. While I was waiting to see him he gave me a pair of giant headphones and asked me if I liked the Rolling Stones. I said I didn't know them. When he came back he realised that he'd forgotten to press play on his cassette deck.' **A Curator**

 Number of floodlights needed to illuminate the 5th Cheshire County Jamboree in 2006; more than 3,000 Scouts from the area took part

SHOP SMART

Ten shops who could kit you out as a Scout, as published in the *Headquarters Gazette*, July 1909 to December 1910:

Adamson & Barlow
Scouts' Outfitters
17 Oxford Street, Bolton

Uniforms (Wholesale)
Messrs Buch,
Manchester

FB Bedford,
Scouts' Outfitters
Silver Street, Bedford

Messrs Dunn
Scouts' Outfitters,
1 Central Buildings,
Sea-side Road, Easbourne

Messrs Dunhill
Scouts' Outfitters
145 Euston Road,
London NW

Davis
Scouts' Outfitters
Arcade, Walsall

Fred, French
Scouts' Outfitters
Fylde Road, Preston
Sample post free. Send for list.

Lewis of Hyland
Scouts' Outfitters
Folkestone

Alec Watson
Scouts' Outfitters
39 Piccadilly
Manchester

W Bell
Scouts' Outfitters
103 Micklegate, York

THINGS ALL SCOUTS SHOULD KNOW

In everyday life, both in town and country,
there are interesting 'signs' to test your scoutcraft...
from *The Scout*, No 1, Volume I, 30 July 1910

Keeps it cool

One of the difficulties often experienced by Scouts when in camp is to keep their supply of butter fresh and firm. If, next time you are in camp, you adopt the following method, you will be able to overcome this difficulty. First get an ordinary unglazed flower-pot and a plate and saucer. Thoroughly clean them, leaving them to soak in cold water for one or two hours. Then place the inverted saucer in the plate, pour a little cold water in the latter, but not enough to touch the butter, which should be placed upon the saucer.

The flower-pot, turned upside down, should be placed over the saucer, so that it rests on the plate, thus making a cover with an airhole at the top. The articles used should always be kept clean.

Number of countries represented in the World Organisation of Scouting in 1990 – World Scout Environment Year

WHOSE BADGE IS IT ANYWAY?

You might have a full arm of new badges. Or you may be taking a trip down memory lane. But can you guess what this Cub Scout Proficiency Badge is for?

a) Timekeeper
b) Navigator
c) Explorer

Answer on page 153.

WE'RE SMOKIN'!

If you're stuck on a desert island, sending smoke signals may be the only way to try and call for help, as long as you can make a fire first, of course. Smoke signals – of the Native American kind – can be made by wafting a blanket, or your last remaining clothes, over the fire. The signal must be visible to the receiver, so make sure you climb a hill or mountain first before you part with any essential kit. There is no standard code for viewing smoke signals – as enemies can also see them so there would be no point – with a few exceptions to the rule. In emergencies:

Blow: Two puffs of smoke *To say:* 'Everything is OK.'
Blow: Three puffs of smoke *To say:* 'Help! Something is wrong.'

The latter is a standard smoke signal used by the Boy Scouts of America to be used by Scouts who are in trouble in the great outdoors. It is taken very seriously and should only be used if something is genuinely wrong. The three-puff rule can also be applied to three gun shots, three whistles or three fires burning at the same time. Just remember not to put yourself in further danger by starting bigger fires than you can handle.

 The number, which when counting on one's fingers in its binary code form (0010000100) will isolate the middle fingers – a fact no Scout should know

PROVE YOUR PROFICIENCY

Bagging a Boy Scout Proficiency Badge circa 1909 could be harder than you think.

To wear a **Carpenter** Badge, you must be able to...

- Shute and glue a 4ft straight joint
- Make a housing, tenon, mortice and halved joint
- Grind and set a chisel and plain iron
- Make a 3ft x 1ft 6in x 1ft 6in dove-tailed lock box, or a table or chair

GUIDE ME TO THE MOON TREES

In July 2005, *BBC News* ran a report on Moon Trees following a broadcast about the phenomenon a week earlier. It pertained to a rediscovery of a 'Moon Tree' in 1997, where a student at Cannelton Elementary School in Indiana told the story of a 'neat tree' at her Girl Scout camp that had supposedly come from the moon. Some might say this tale was bordering on lunacy and, in effect, they would be right: these are trees with a lunar history, those that were grown from seeds which journeyed to the moon and back on board *Apollo 14* in 1971. When a teacher at Cannelton Elementary began to probe into the history of Moon Trees, she found that seeds were germinated and planted as part of the US bicentennial celebrations in 1976. The seeds had been taken into space by Stuart Roosa, an astronaut on *Apollo 14*. He choose them as the one ingredient of his 'personal preference kit' – a sock-sized pouch that *Apollo* astronauts were allowed to fill with their prize possessions. Nearly 500 seeds made the journey but the first attempt to grow them back home failed. Many thought that the harsh radiation had rendered them incapable of growth. But second attempts by various institutions – schools, government agencies and Boy and Girl Scout Troops – around the US did produce results. Compared with Earth Trees – those grown from their twin seeds (those that were born of the same mother and father of the Moon Tree, but without the lunar experience), the results showed that there was no difference in the germination process that took hold. While no record was kept of who got Moon Tree seeds, it is known that some got as far as the UK. Second – or even third – generation seeds can now be bought from the US (customs regulations permitting) from a company called American Forests. So if you do see a Moon Tree around – maybe at your local Scout Pack Meeting Place or at Scout Camp – you'll know it's not a moment of complete lunacy.

Number of countries who had visited the Scout website
www.scoutbase.org.uk in the two years since it was set up in 1996

QUOTE UNQUOTE

Hump your own pack.
Canadian saying as cited in reference to 'Happiness and Success' by Robert Baden-Powell in *Rovering to Success: A Book of Life-Sport for Young Men*, 1930

WHAT A DAY

The date 22 February is well known to Scouts worldwide as Founder's Day in celebration of Baden-Powell's birthday (he was born in 1857).

Coincidentally, 22 February is also the birthday of B-P's wife Olave, the first Chief Guide, although she was born 32 years later in 1889. Her special day is commemorated by Girl Guides and Girl Scouts as Thinking Day. And just when you thought that was just about enough for one day, here are a few more happenings that 22 February can claim for itself...

1,295BC: The coronation of Ramses II, on whose face the sun's rays fall each year in Abu Simbel temple.

1281: Martin IV becomes Pope.

1288: Nicholas IV becomes Pope.

1879: Frank Woolworth opens the first of many stores, in New York.

1924: Calvin Coolidge becomes the first president of the United States to deliver a radio broadcast from the White House.

1956: Elvis Presley enters the music charts for the first time, with 'Heartbreak Hotel'.

1969: The last time all four Beatles are together for a recording session.

1997: In Roslin, Scotland, scientists announce that an adult sheep named Dolly had been successfully cloned.

2006: At least six men stage Britain's biggest ever robbery, stealing £53m from a Securitas depot in Tonbridge, Kent.

The following people share the same birthday as Olave and B-P: Charles VII of France (1403); George Washington, first president of the US (1732); Luis Bunuel, Spanish-born film director (1900); Sir John Mills, British actor (1908); Renato Dulbecco, Nobel Prize winner for physiology (1914); Edward Gorey, US illustrator (1925); Kenneth Williams, British actor (1926); Bruce Forsyth, British entertainer (1928); Ted Kennedy, US senator (1932); Julie Walters, British actress (1950); Tim Young, Canadian ice-hockey player (1955); Kyle MacLachlan, US actor (1959); James Blunt, British musician and Chris Moyles, British DJ (1974); Drew Barrymore, US actress (1975).

 Degrees Fahrenheit of the second-hottest temperature recorded, in Death Valley, California, 1913 – something weather-mad Scouts should know

RUN WITH THE PACK

Sign	Name	Call	Colours
	Peewit	Whistle – *'Peewit'*	Green and White
	Wood-Pigeon	Call – *'Book-booroo'*	Blue and Grey
	Cuckoo	Call – *'Cook-koo'*	Grey
	Lion	Call – *'Eu-ugh'*	Yellow and Red
	Kangaroo	Australian – *'Coo-ee'*	Red and Grey

THE MEANING OF SCOUT

According to the *Collins New English Dictionary*, 1962:

scout (skout) ***n.*** a person sent out to reconnoiter; a look-out; a Boy Scout; a ship used for reconnoitering; a reconnaissance aeroplane; a road patrolman of the Automobile Association or the Royal Automobile Club; a college man-servant at Oxford; one who fields in cricket; *–v.t.* to reconnoiter; to spy out; to perform the activities of the Boy Scout organisation. **–scout'ing** ***n.*** reconnaissance; activities of the Boy Scouts. **–scout'craft** ***n.*** the art of scouting; a comprehensive term for the various activities associated with the Boy Scouts. **–scout'master** ***n.*** adult instructor and organiser in the Boy Scouts [I.fr. escoute, fr. Escouter, to listen].
[to jut out].

scout (skout) ***n.*** a high rock [O.N. skuta]

scout (skout) ***v.t.*** to reject with contempt; to dismiss from the mind as too absurd; to sneer at; to ridicule; to flout.–scout'ingly adv. [etym. Uncertain].

FIRST NIGHTS AWAY

Days and nights away at Scout camp, as outlined by EE Reynolds in *Boy Scout Jubilee*, 1957 (Oxford University Press). One wonders what kind of activity 'signs, calls, sluts' could be:

Mon	Meet 10am, pitch tent	Finish preparation	Explore. Bed 8pm each night
Tue	Rise 5am, parade dispatch running	Climbing and war dance*	Off 6-7.30pm
Wed	Rise 5am, flag-raising	Signs, calls, sluts	Knots, rations
Thur	Rise 5am, cooking, judge distance	Fishing	Rifle practice
Fri	Rise 5am, huts, tracking	Target, war dance	Climbing
Sat	Rise 5am, storming	Compass, rifle, Scouts meets Scout	Cooking
Sun	Rise 5am, service, hour off	Service, walk	Knots, rations
Mon	Rise 5am, fishing	Dispatch run, ambulance	Climbing, knots
Tue	Rise 5am, general cleaning up	Take tent down and pack	Start home
WET DAY	Rise 5am Kim's game, cards		Knots etc, off 6-7pm

* The Eengonyâma Chorus

NOTES FROM THE FOUNDER

B-P on garters...

Another insignificant and yet important item of the Scout uniform is the Honi Soit part of it – the garters. These are intended not only to do the useful job of keeping the stockings from slipping down but actually skeins of the same wool they supply the mending material for repairing holes as these occur. The tabs at the end are coloured to distinguish the grade of the wearer, red for Rover Scouts and green for Scouts.

***Lessons from the Varsity of Life*,**
Robert Baden-Powell, 1933

 Number of countries worldwide that are represented by the World Association of Girl Guides and Girl Scouts (WAGGGS)

KEY SCOUTING DATES: 1980s

1981

March Because of the rising number of people without a job a special 'Scouting and Unemployment' scheme is introduced.

July 500 Venture Scouts acts as torchbearers at the royal fireworks in Hyde Park, as part of the wedding celebrations of the Prince and Princess of Wales.

1986

April Beaver Scouts introduced.

1989

June The result of a uniform consultation results in the abolition of headgear for all Sections.

CELEBRITY SCOUTS: DAVID GILMOUR, SYD BARRETT & TIM RENWICK, PINK FLOYD

What these famous Scouts did next...

The legendary band Pink Floyd seem an unlikely hotbed of former Scouts, but at the pinnacle of their greatness, their ranks included not one, but three former members of 'the Movement'. Perhaps the most surprising Scout was Roger Keith 'Syd' Barrett. Best known from his drug-fuelled demise from dementia, and lamented death in 2006, the far-out lyricist was in fact a Scout Patrol Leader. Syd met ace guitarist David Gilmour as a child when growing up in Cambridge, and while they certainly shared a wealth of common interests and pastimes, they are not known to have Scouted together. Not so for Tim Renwick, however. The second guitarist who would be brought into the band later, served under the authority of Syd's Scout Patrol leadership and this is how they first met. The band's album *Dark Side of the Moon* is said to be the third most successful of all time and the band were inducted into the US Rock and Roll Hall of Fame in 1996; whether any of this success can be attributed to skills acquired at the Scouts has not been confirmed, although *Scouting for Boys* does appear in the song 'Welcome to the Machine'. David Gilmour is well known for his ongoing devotion to 'good turns': as vice-president of the homeless charity Crisis, to whom he donated £3.6 million from the sale of his London house in 2003. From band practice in a Scout hut, Perne Road in Cambridgeshire (when in earlier band The Newcomers) to top billing at Live 8, he's living proof that Scouts can grow up to be cool after all.

CRACK THE CODE

Can you work out the Morse code message below, without cheating by using the reference on page 39?

-... .-. --- .-- -. ... . .- / .. ... .-.. .- -. -..

Clue: First call to camp.

Answer on page 153.

THE CAMP COOK: ONE MAN STEW (PERFECT FOR CANNIBALS)

From *Backwoods Cooking – Practical Methods and Recipes*, a reprint of a popular collection that first appeared in *Scouting* magazine.

You will need:

- 1 potato
- 1 carrot
- 1 onion
- 1 cup mincemeat
- 1 stock cube
- Salt and pepper to taste

Method:

1. Peel and slice the potato, carrot and onion. Sprinkle salt and pepper, if required, onto the vegetables.
2. Form a double-thickness layer of foil into a dish and place a layer of potato in the bottom. The meat, carrots and onions can be added in alternate layers on top of the potato.
3. Sprinkle a stock cube over the vegetables and add water to cover.
4. Place a sheet of foil over the vegetables, and place the dish onto hot embers. Cook for approximately 40 minutes. *Serves one.*

QUOTE UNQUOTE

Rain? Cold? Yes, I suppose they come, but you really get to disregard them when you are in the regular swing and habit of weekend camping.

Robert Baden-Powell on 'The Joy of the Open Road' in *Rovering to Success: A Book of Life-Sport for Young Men*, 1930

GIFTS FOR GARTERS

'Appropriate Xmas Presents for Scouts' as per an advertisement for Wm, Good & Son (52, King William St, London EC4) in the *Headquarters Gazette*, December 1920:

Hand-signalling lamps, solid oak cases

Tappers • Electric torches • First aid cases

Officers' water bottles (suitable for presentation to Scoutmasters)

Buzzers • Wrist compasses • Knives

Boxing gloves, youth sizes

Footballs, full-size • Footballs, small sizes

Meccano • Conjuring tricks

Jigsaw puzzles, in boxes containing 100 pieces

Jigsaw puzzles, in boxes containing 80 pieces

Table games, ludo, snakes and ladders,
halma, tiddleywinks, etc.

CELEBRITY SCOUTS: DAVID BECKHAM

What this famous Scout did next...

David Robert Joseph Beckham, began his working life collecting glasses at Walthamstow Dog Track for £10 a night. But, with true Scout zeal, this wasn't a boy to give up the game just yet. At the height of his fame he would play football for Manchester United and Real Madrid, become the fifth most capped England player of all time, captain of the England team and only the fifth player in World Cup history to score twice from direct free kicks. Fans who want to trace his steps to fame quite literally can follow the recently ordained 'Beckham Way'. The trail begins at Whipps Cross Hospital maternity wing, includes a pitch at Peter May Sports Centre (when he played for the under-10s here, he scored more than 100 goals in three seasons) and raises a toast to Gilwell Park – the present-day Scout headquarters – where he went camping with the Cub Scouts. Perhaps this is where 'Golden Balls' got his taste for adorning his body with emblems, although tribute tattoos are taking things one thing further than a couple of Activity Badges. Although 2006 did see Beckham's departure from the England squad following a forgettable World Cup team performance, the man surely still deserves his stripes: in the Scouts' case, honorary badges for Sports Enthusiast, Physical Recreation and the highly esteemed Fitness Challenge.

Number of portraits Queen Elizabeth II has sat for, the last being painted by former Scout and campfire song champion Rolf Harris in 2005

AN A-Z OF ACTIVITY BADGES: R-Z

This most up-to-date list of Scout Activity Badges proves there's more than one reason to join the Scouts. The list is provided in bit-sized pieces throughout the book so as not to get badge addicts too over-excited.

- Smallholder
- Snowsports
- Sports Enthusiast
- Street Sports – New!
- Survival Skills
- Swimming (staged)
- Water Sports
- World Faiths
- Writer

Note: We must admit this is not a true A-Z, due to the current absence of any badges that start with a 'Z'.

BADEN-POWELL THE SPY

One day a war hero, the next caught and shot as a German spy! In his book *Lessons from the Varsity of Life*, Baden-Powell reported, with some humour, on how he was once lampooned as a spy by the American press.

In his account he quotes an initial cable to the papers as saying that: 'Baden-Powell shot in Tower of London as German spy upon return from Germany. Was caught with maps of fortifications which he was trying to dispose of to the enemy. Mr Walterbury, returning from Pittsburgh, tells of the above knowledge gleaned from brother, an English office who was present at the trial and saw him shot to death.' The consequent newspaper account in a Pittsburg paper headlined with 'BADEN-POWELL SHOT AS A SPY' and continued with a detailed account of Baden's execution, where he 'marched to his place of execution without a quiver'. Although the accusation was the heaviest there could be at the time, the account did however hail him as 'one of the bravest soldiers who ever headed her armies in foreign lands'. Baden-Powell took his new status with good humour, secure in the knowledge that he wasn't in Germany during the war, and secretly pleased to receive such a glorious epitaph while still alive. He believed the rumour may have come from the War Office who sometimes leaked fake 'confidential' information to see 'how far the hare would run'.

 Number of street – 140th street – also known as Girl Scout Road, off State Highway 23, named the 'Country Music Highway' of the US

HOW TO MAKE A TENT

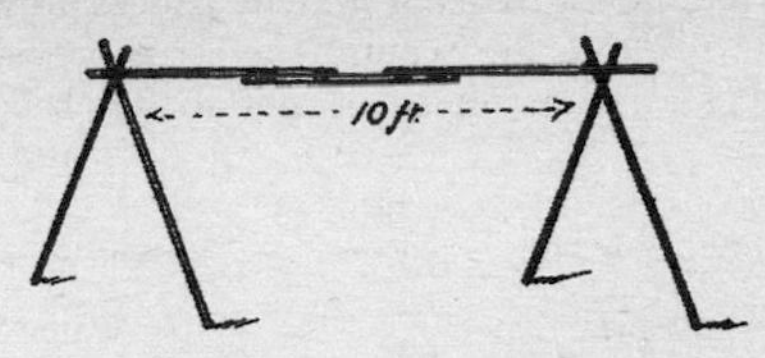

Frame of six Scout's staves and an extra joint to lengthen ridge pole.

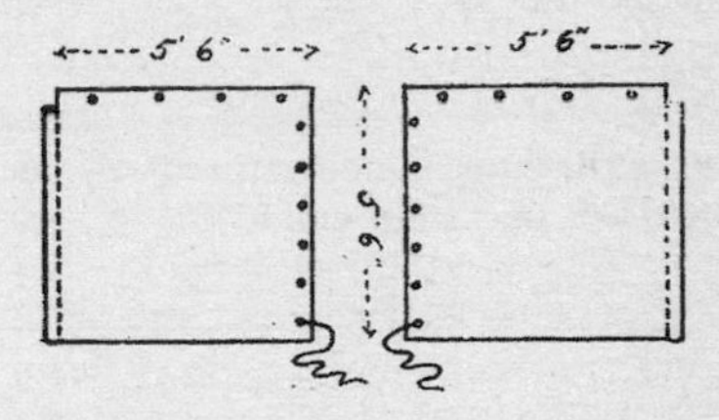

Six squares of canvas, 5ft 6in square, with cyclets and hemmed tube on one side. Each Scout carries one, and can pack his kit in it if necessary, or use it as a cape in rain.

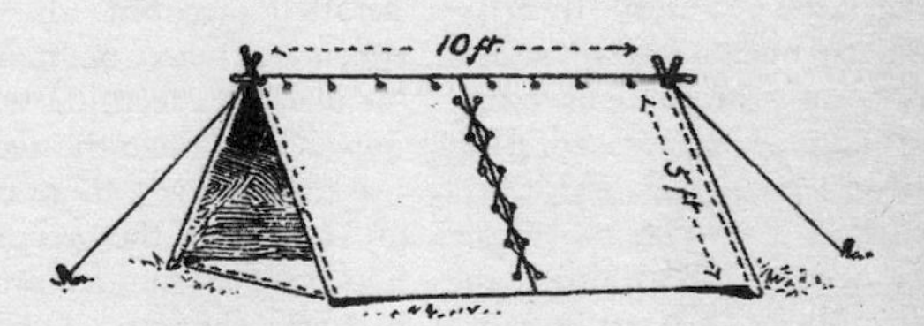

Boy Scout's tent for a Patrol. Four canvas squares make the tent. Two make the ground sheet.

QUOTE UNQUOTE

To me [the Scouts] was how to set fire to things.
I've been setting fire to things all my life.
Anthony Worrall Thompson,
restaurateur and former Scout

Number of euphemisms for the word 'drunk' found on the BBC's E-cyclopedia in March 2002 – none of which a good Scout should be

KEY SCOUTING DATES: 1990s

1990

February The decision is made in principle for The Scout Association to become fully co-educational and to allow girls to join the Beaver, Cub and Scout sections.

1996

October The Scout Association's first website – www.scoutbase.org.uk – is launched.

QUOTE UNQUOTE

Oh, I see that all right, but what I mean is, Edwin would do it so much better than I would. These Boy Scouts are up to all sorts of dodges. They spoor, don't you know, and take cover and creep about, and what not.

Bertie Wooster in PG Wodehouse's *Carry on Jeeves*, 1925

SCOUTING AROUND: NEW ZEALAND, AUCKLAND

In January 1912, Baden-Powell set off on his first world tour to see how the Scout Movement was developing. He recorded and later published his observations and musings. Today there are more than 28 million Scouts, youth and adults, boys and girls in 216 countries and territories. Of these, around 19,751 are from New Zealand.

I shall not easily forget my first view of the New Zealand boys; it was a fine sight, for 3,000 Cadets and 400 Boy Scouts were drawn up in a sort of natural arena in the park on the heights overlooking Auckland, and 10,000 spectators were on the surrounding slopes. With bands playing and colour flying they made a brave show, and they seemed to be as good as they looked.

The Boy Scouts has a very large number of badges of efficiency, and one of the Auckland troops, the 1st Devonport, were the winners of the King's Flag, having 23 King's Scouts in their ranks!

...And you should hear their 'Haka' that is the New Zealand edition of the 'Eengonyâma' salute! A leader starts the chant, they all smack their thighs and stamp in time and... the effect is fine.

Robert Baden-Powell,
***Boy Scouts Beyond the Seas: My World Tour,* 1913**

 Number of the 214 former and present astronauts who have taken part in Scouting; including Neil Armstrong

BRING BACK BROWNSEA

All the camp kit you need for recreating Baden-Powell's experimental Scout camp (deriving from the original list of items each of the 20 original attendees were asked to bring with them):

Knife, fork and spoon
Two enamelled plates and one mug
Waterproof sheet
Two blankets (no sheets)
One pillow and pillowcase
Two rough towels
One smooth towel
Tin cooking 'Billy' *
Canvas haversack *
Two coat straps, 8in long *
Jack knife and lanyard *
Soap and sponge
Toothbrush
Brush and comb
Small looking glass

* *Optional. Can be bought in camp at low price if desired.*

SCOUTS FOR PEACE: CROATIA

Scouting isn't just one big carefree Jamboree. With its inclusive approach to all nations, countries and cultures, the Scout Movement has helped many people in war-torn countries over the years, some of which were described in *Scouting* magazine, July 2000...

Zora, a psychologist, first came into contact with Scouting in 1993. She took part in the Croatian Scouts' sunrise movement that offered war-traumatised children and teenagers the chance to camp with Scouts, both boys and girls of their own age, to help free themselves from fear and anguish and to learn again how to live with others. She worked with children who had lost all interest in life, those who had lost family and friends in the war, and young people who still suffered from nightmares because of their experiences. Young Scouts came from all over Europe to help with the project, and in time the shattered children they were working with began to laugh again and found themselves enjoying new responsibilities.

Internet slang for 'I love you', being the letter count for each word in the sequence of the phrase – perhaps a little strong for the JOTI

NOTES FROM THE FOUNDER

B-P on air-raids...

During the Great War the police in London took on a large number of Scouts to help them in air raids. They only took those who had earned the Bugler's Badge – because they wanted them to go round the streets as soon as an air raid was over to sound the call "All clear," so that people would come out of their houses and shelters again.

This meant that so soon as an air raid was on the boys had to get into uniform and go to their police stations ready for duty just at a time when other people were taking shelter.

When I called for volunteers for this duty, I expected that very few would be allowed by their parents to take it up or would care to do it themselves on account of the danger. But not a bit of it! They came forward in their hundreds, keen to do their bit and to show their pluck, and their parents were equally keen that they should do so. As one mother said: "If Jimmy has got to be killed, much better that he should be killed doing something useful for other people."

I expect very few bugler Scouts imagined, when they first learned to blow the bugle, that it was going to be the means of their doing duty for the country and winning the War Service Badge for real service against an enemy.

Robert Baden-Powell, *Adventuring to Manhood*, 1936

THE CAMP COOK: CHRISTMAS PUDDING

From *Backwoods Cooking – Practical Methods and Recipes*, a reprint of a popular collection that first appeared in *Scouting* magazine.

You will need:

- Bread
- Butter or margarine
- Currants, sultanas
- Oranges and apples

Method:

1. Take one slice of bread per person and butter one side, laying that side down onto two layers of foil.
2. Prepare a mixture of dried fruits, grated orange peel, sliced apples and oranges, sugar and butter or margarine.
3. Spread this thickly onto the bread, place another slice on the top, and butter the top of the sandwich.
4. Wrap in the foil and place on embers for about eight minutes per side.

Although not a traditional Christmas pudding recipe, served with cream it makes a very tasty dessert!

 Number of countries and territories represented at Baden-Powell House Scout Activity Centre on 1 April 2006

THINGS ALL SCOUTS SHOULD KNOW

In everyday life, both in town and country,
there are interesting 'signs' to test your scoutcraft...
from *The Scout*, No 1, Volume I, 16 May 1908

Saves boot leather

- A good dodge is in use among many of those whose occupation necessitates continual digging. A piece of iron is placed underneath the boot and fastened on by a strap.

- This iron not only prevents the centre of the boot from wearing so quickly, but saves a good deal of jarring which is produced when the fork of the spade is stamped on.

CELEBRITY SCOUTS: JARVIS COCKER

What this famous Scout did next...

Born Jarvis Branson Cocker on 19 September 1963, the bespectacled frontman of Britpop band Pulp is not a man to forget his roots – and that includes his old Cub Scout Pack. On receiving a triple platinum disc for the album *Different Class* he promptly donated it to the 270th Scout Group in Sheffield after bumping into Cub Scout Leader Irene Percival in a London supermarket. The disc could then be auctioned off to help raise funds for the Pack. According to one 1998 interview on www.acrylicafternoons.com, a site dedicated to anything and everything Pulp, Jarvis is unabashedly forthcoming about his Scouting days: 'It was good was Scouts, when you went camping out and that. It was a good laugh.' He does admit to telling everyone his name was 'John' for a whole week at Cub Scout camp, however, in fear that the outing of real name 'Jarvis' would make his life hell. Launched to fame at music festival and camping 'experience' Glastonbury in 1995, it seems his experiences at Cub Scouts have stood him in good stead. Follow-up works have included more Pulp albums, music videos for Aphex Twin and Nightmares on Wax, a string of collaborations with the likes of Nancy Sinatra and Charlotte Gainsbourg, plus three tracks for the film *Harry Potter and the Goblet of Fire*. His choices for Radio 4's Desert Island Discs in 2005 could be seen to reflect the romanticism of the perpetual Scout within, including Robert Mellin's 'The Adventures of Robinson Crusoe' and a track by the Patrol Leader-sounding Lieutenant Pigeon. But some mod cons are welcome: Jarvis's 'luxury item' of 'bed and mosquito net' reveals that he may have moved on from the bivouac.

QUOTE UNQUOTE

Assume the worst: the pessimistic ones are worth their weight in gold on expeditions.
Sir Ranulph Fiennes, explorer and former Scout

HOW TO WEAR THE ORIGINAL SCOUT UNIFORM

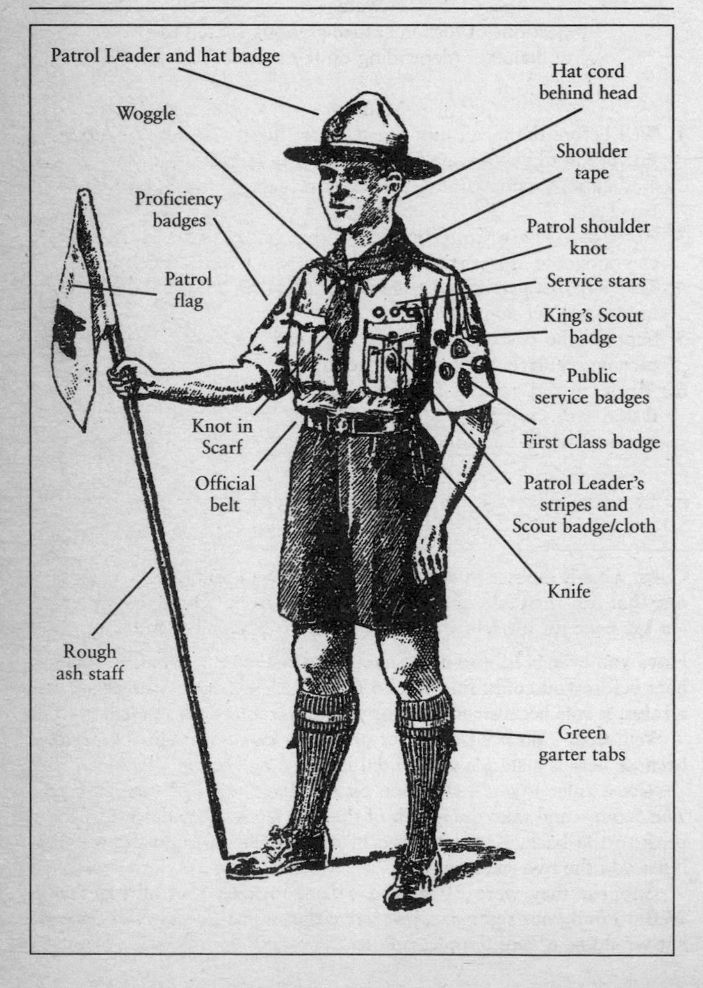

 Number in millions of children suffering from malnutrition and repeated disease by a 2006 Unicef report – something all Scouts should know

THE CAMP COOK: EDIBLE BOWLS

From *Backwoods Cooking – Practical Methods and Recipes*, a reprint of a popular collection that first appeared in *Scouting* magazine.

You will need:

- Two cups plain flour
- One cup of fat
- One level dessertspoon baking powder
- Pinch of salt
- Water
- Sections of logs, measuring about 10cm (4in) in diameter (depending on the size of the bowl)

Method:

1. Well before the meal, mix together the flour, fat, salt and baking powder until you have a breadcrumb-like mixture.
2. Add enough water to produce a stiff dough, divide it and roll into two balls.
3. Remove the bark from the ends of the chosen logs and seal them as you would a greenstick by holding them over flames briefly.
4. Take a ball of pastry and mould it around the end of a log, pressing in into a bowl shape.
5. Support the pastry, still on the log, and cook over hot embers, turning regularly until golden brown.
6. When cooked, remove from the logs and allow them to cool. The dishes will certainly only last for one meal, holding sweet or savoury meals – and they can be eaten afterwards. *Makes two.*

IF THE CAP FITS!

Cubs, what is the size of your cap? If you've had problems getting the one that fits, then take the following advice from 'The Cubs' Corner – a big page for big fellows' in *The Scout*, 9 November 1929...

Have you ever been into a hat shop, and had to try on half a dozen hats before you could find one to fit you? If you have been through all this, it was because you forgot your correct size, wasn't it?

Well, there's no need to forget or not to know your size in future because here is a simple way to tell it.

Get a ruler – you'll find one on the back cover of this copy of *The Scout* – and take the length of the hat, from the underside of the peak to the back. Keep this size in mind, then measure the width. Now add the two sizes together.

Suppose they were 7½in and 5½in, making 13in all together. Well, to find your right size, just halve that number. The size of your hat would be 6½in! Simple, isn't it?

Placement number of the country Georgia in the World Organisation of the Scout Movement (WOSM); they joined WOSM in 1997

FUN FOR FREE

Christmas 1980 was a grim time for many people in the UK, as the recession took the nation in the full strength of its grip. For many children of families who were affected, the Scouts provided a welcome source of relief. In the Cub Scout supplement of *Scouting* magazine the same year, the following 'Christmas Challenge' was published in a bid to keep flagging spirits up and days filled during the school break. No money was required:

- Make a collage using old Christmas cards and wrapping paper.
- Make something useful from gift boxes or odds and ends.
- Cook a simple meal using leftovers.
- Make daily weather recordings e.g. rainfall, snowfall, sunshine, wind direction.
- Chart traffic increase over holiday–suggest 1 hour morning or afternoon. Identify any plants or wildlife visible at this time of year.
- Carry out a good turn selected by yourself.
- Show someone else how to play a new game received at Christmas.
- Write a thank you letter, either on behalf of the Pack or on yourself.
- Take part in a Patrol Activity.
- Find out a local place of interest.
- Do a survey on prices of goods in shops–perhaps a new item of equipment needed in the Pack.
- Was there any difference in price after Christmas?

ALL MAPPED OUT

Some Scouts sew their badges onto their sleeves (the picture on page 146 should give a clear indication of where they are supposed to go, for those not in the know). Some Scouts sew their badges on blankets (you can pretty much position these where you wish, but maybe place the ones you like best near the top so you can see them). And some Scouts – namely the 2nd Little Heath Cubs of Hertfordshire – embraced Baden-Powell's passion for a spot of needlework, and sewed some 780 District badges into a map of the UK. Beg, borrow or steal, the badges at first came in from far and wide. By July 2006, they had received around 700 of the required badges, with some help from the International Badgers Club (a slightly more cajoling group, who collect Scout badges from all over the world). It was a push, but by October that same year, they had them all. Cub Scout Leader Charles Dace (not to be confused with Charles Dance) was thrilled with his Cub Scouts. Monies raised by auctioning the map on eBay were donated to Scouts from the less fortunate countries of Lesotho and Swaziland, so that they could attend the 2007 World Scout Jamboree.

 Number of pages packed with games in Robert Baden-Powell's book Scouting Games, *published in 1910*

KEY SCOUTING DATES: 2000s

2001

February New logo is launched. New uniform is launched during London Fashion Week.

2002

February Explorer Scouts and the Scout Network are introduced.

2004

July Current Chief Scout, Peter Duncan (formerly of *Blue Peter*) is appointed to the post.

2005

July-August The UK hosts EuroJam, a Jamboree for the European region.

2007

July-August Centenary celebrations get into full swing with the Scouting's Sunrise and the 21st World Scout Jamboree.

QUOTE UNQUOTE

Marry an outdoors woman. Then if you throw her out into the yard on a cold night, she can still survive.
WC Fields, US actor and writer

FANCY DRESS THAT!

Dressing-up pointers for the Pack pantomime, from 'The Cubs' Corner – a big page for big fellows' in *The Scout*, 16 November 1929...

Quite a lot of Packs will be holding a pack pantomime or Christmas concert in the next two or three weeks and these can be made all the more jolly if the costumes are made by the Cubs themselves. Here are just a few ideas which will help you to think of others:

- A Santa Claus beard can be made from cotton wool hung by thread or wire over the ears.
- Imitation jewellery can be made from cocoa tins – the tins being crimpled into different shapes and given a dab of enamel here and there.
- An old bowler hat, the brim cut off, painted with gold or silver paint, and a feather stuck in the side, makes an excellent helmet for a fairy prince.
- A loaf of bread can be disguised as a cooked chicken in a Christmas dinner scene.

SCOUT'S HORROR: A TIGHT FIX

No *Scout's Companion* would be complete without a few Scouting nightmares, sad yarns, odd tales and wicked deeds, just to balance the books. The tellers of these anecdotes wish to remain anonymous just in case the Scouts come and make them do some good turns.

'I think I only earned about three badges. I remember one was "Home Help" or something. You had to make a meal, clean your house, sew on a button... That was probably it. Everyone had this badge – it was the easiest. When we went to camps and Gang Shows we'd see other Cubs with dozens of badges on both sleeves – we thought they were a bit strange. "Bob-a-Job" was really embarrassing. I remember clearing moss from between the bricks of my friend's mum's patio for about 50p. I never earned very much. I think my mum discouraged me from doing it, because in her mind it was begging. I remember doing shoe-shining outside Safeway. I got polish all over an elderly lady's tan tights by mistake. She didn't seem to mind.'
A Curator

FROM THE GRAVE

On 8 January 1941, Robert Baden-Powell, Chief Scout of the world, died. The following day he received the following obituary in *The Times*: 'If any of us were asked to name the man, or the woman, who in our lifetime rendered the greatest service to the rising generation, we should find it difficult to find an alternative to Lord Baden-Powell. The creation of the Boy Scouts – with their counterpart the Girl Guides – was his work and his alone... What is perfectly certain is that no one but Baden-Powell could have conceived it in all its details and carried it into effect with such amazing success that, from small beginnings in this country, the Boy Scout Movement has long since captured the whole Empire and indeed the whole world.'

His grave in the tiny cemetery of Nyeri, Kenya, where he would spend many of his final days, was marked by a simple stone – it carried his name and the Boy Scout trail sign for 'I have gone home', a circle with a dot inside.

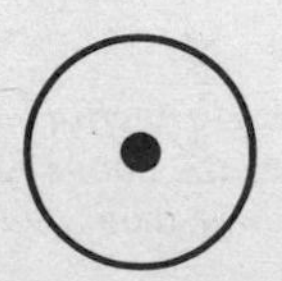

 Birthday of Robert Baden-Powell, if he was still alive on 22 February 2007 – the date was celebrated by some 28 million Scouts around the world

DURING THE COMPILATION OF THIS BOOK, THE COMPANION TEAM...

Tried to navigate their way around the world with just a compass and the North Star.

Learned how not to put a tent up when the rain came in.

Survived on a diet of eggs in oranges and beans in a billy can.

Wouldn't leave the house without at least one badge on.

Started sending text messages in Morse code that no one else could understand.

Tried to make fire with two sticks but ended up with blisters instead.

Started running in packs and howling at the moon.

Tried to do one good turn, well, nearly every day.

Tried to be prepared but still managed to forget many vital things.

Dressed up as Pocahontas and called it working.

Got repetitive strain from all that saluting.

Wondered about the true wearability of woggles.

Brought traffic to a standstill while practising semaphore.

Got caught out while impersonating an owl.

Paddled their own canoes.

But most importantly, had a right old Jamboree doing the whole camp thing.

Please note that although every effort has been made to ensure the accuracy of this book, the above facts may be the result of too much fun, frivolity and fresh air.

Some say why don't you be a Scout, why don't you read a book? But I get much more pleasure when I'm playing on me uke.
George Formby, musician

152 *Distance in km of the West Highland Way, a long-distance footpath in Scotland that all Scouts should walk along*

ANSWERS

The answers. As if you needed them.

P.17. They are all Patrol names.

P23. They're all original Wolf Cub Scout badges.

P26. Baden-Powell.

P41. Dragon boating.

P49. They're all orienteering terms.

P.51. Jamboree.

P59. Air-spotter.

P72. The Boy Scouts.

P76. Fire safety.

P88. They're all types of knot.

P92. Artist.

P103. Ging Gang Goolie.

P107. Boatswain.

P116. Gilwell Park.

P132. Explorer.

P138. Brownsea Island.

Distance in miles, plus a hundred, of the Boy Scouts of America hiking trail 'The Silver Moccasin Trail' of which the highest point is Mount Baden-Powell

BIBLIOGRAPHY

MAGAZINE/PERIODICALS

Boy Scouts (Baden Powell's) Headquarters Gazette: Issues/volumes: July 1909 to Dec 1910; December 1920.

The Scout: Issues/volumes: No 1, No 1, Vol, 1; August 29, 1908; May 14, 1910; November 9, 1929; November 16, 1929; October 13, 1949; October 14 1939; October 27, 1949; March 2, 1950; May 4, 1950; June 29, 1950.

Scouting: Issues/volumes: 1970; 1980; November 1990; July 2000.

The Scouter: Issues/volumes: 1920 (August); 1930; Volume XXXIV, 1940; 1950; 1960.

BOOKS

Adventuring to Manhood, Lord Baden-Powell of Gilwell

Backwoods Cooking – Practical Methods and Recipes, Eddie Greenhalgh, David Easton and Doug Mountford (previously published in *Scouting* magazine)

Boy Scouts Beyond the Seas 'My World Tour', Sir Robert Baden-Powell, K.C.B. Illustrated by the author's own sketches

Boy Scout Jubilee, E. E. Reynolds

Carry on Jeeves, PG Wodehouse

Footsteps of the Founder – Lord Baden Powell, Compiled and edited by Mario Sica

Handbook for Boys, Boy Scouts of America

Lessons from the Varsity of Life, Lord Baden-Powell of Gilwell

Life's Snags and How to Meet Them, Lord Baden-Powell

Official History of Scouting

Paddle Your Own Canoe or Tips for boys – From the Jungle and Elsewhere, Lord Baden-Powell of Gilwell

Rovering to Success – A book of Life-Sport for Young Men, Lord Baden Powell

Sport in War, Maj.Gen.R.S.S. Baden-Powell

The Adventures of a Spy [first published as *My Adventures as a Spy*, 1915], Lord Baden-Powell of Gilwell

The Jungle Book, Rudyard Kipling

OTHER MEDIA

100 Years of Scouting: The Official Scout Centenary DVD, The Scout Association

INDEX

10 THINGS YOU MAY NOT KNOW ABOUT SCOUTING

1. Scouting is for girls as well as boys
Girls and young women make up almost 10 per cent of the Movement in the UK, constituting one of our biggest development areas. We are the country's largest mixed organisation for young people.

2. Scouting is a global movement
Scouting is active in more than 216 countries and territories with more than 28 million Members worldwide.

3. Young people can join at any stage of their development
If you are aged between 6 and 25, then you can start Scouting almost immediately. You do not have to have been a Cub to be a Scout. We welcome late starters!

4. The Scout Association is a registered charity
The Scout Association is a non-profit organisation that supports the work of Scouting in the UK. We work with a number of ethical partners on projects and resources that are beneficial to both the organisation involved and our Members. Donate or find out about sponsorship opportunities.

5. Scouting is great value!
Scouting membership represents outstanding value. With weekly activities including abseiling, canoeing, archery, caving, climbing and karting, there are few other organisations who can offer so much for so little. Typically, a year's Scouting costs less than a single ballet or piano lesson.

6. Robert Baden-Powell, the Founder of Scouting was recently voted the 13th most influential person of the twentieth century.

7. Famous former Scouts include Sir Paul McCartney, Sir David Attenborough, Steven Spielberg and David Beckham
Scouts go on to excel in the worlds of business, sport, entertainment and the media. Our fun, flexible programme helps young people develop team skills, leadership qualities and lasting friendships.

8. Each day 100,000 people in the UK take part in Scouting activities
That's more than the 0_2 arena can hold!

9. *Scouting for Boys*, Baden-Powell's blueprint for the Scout Movement, is one of the most popular books of all time
B-P's famous 1908 book became the publishing phenomenon of the twentieth century, enjoying worldwide sales second only to the Bible. The title was recently re-issued by Oxford University Press.

10. Young people are desperate to join Scouting
One of the biggest myths about Scouting is that Groups are

closing down due to a lack of young people wanting to become Members. Nothing could be further from the truth and we currently have 30,000 young people on our waiting lists simply because we do not have enough adults to help out. As an adult in Scouting you can help out once a week, once a month or even just twice a year. No matter how much time you can spare, or what skills you have, there is a role to suit everyone in Scouting, whether it be working with young people, teaching an activity, acting as treasurer or simply mowing the ground's lawn in the summer.

Be part of the adventure. Visit www.scouts.org.uk/join to find out how you can help or call 0845 300 1818.

THE SCOUT ASSOCIATION

In the UK The Scout Association provides adventurous activities and personal development opportunities for 400,000 girls and boys aged 6-25, of all faiths, backgrounds and religions. We believe that young people develop most when they are 'learning by doing', when they are given responsibility, work in teams, take acceptable risks and think for themselves. As Scouts, young people have the opportunity to try a whole range of activities, from rafting, climbing and sailing to cycling, camping and flying.

The Centenary of Scouting marks 100 years of everyday adventure, of promoting peace, of doing a good turn and, of course, always doing our best. Throughout the year, UK Scouts will be taking part in Centenary projects in their communities to celebrate adventure, international friendship and help change the world for good.

From Scouts summitting Everest to a Jamboree for 40,000 Scouts from almost every country in the world, our 100-year celebrations show just how far the Movement has come and the passion and commitment from those involved. In May, hundreds of thousands of Scouts in the UK are under canvas to promote the outdoor element of Scouting. On 1 August 2007, Scouts of every age from around the UK will join in with 28 million Scouts from around the world to celebrate the dawn of a new Century of Scouting to renew their Scout Promise. There are 'Scout' 50 pence pieces in circulation (check your pocket or purse!), Royal Mail Scout Centenary stamps, television shows dedicated to the Movement plus numerous books published (including this one!) to mark a journey that has helped millions of young people become active members of the community: young people who are self-reliant, caring, responsible, and who show commitment.

Visit **www.scouts.org.uk** to find out about Scouting and the work we do.